ALSO BY TERRELL OWENS

Catch This!: Going Deep with the NFL's Sharpest Weapon
(with Stephen Singular)

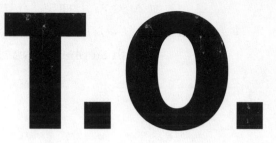

T.O.

TERRELL OWENS

AND JASON ROSENHAUS

SIMON & SCHUSTER
NEW YORK LONDON TORONTO SYDNEY

SIMON & SCHUSTER
Rockefeller Center
1230 Avenue of the Americas
New York, NY 10020

SIMON & SCHUSTER and colophon are registered trademarks
of Simon & Schuster, Inc.

For information about special discounts for bulk purchases,
please contact Simon & Schuster, Special Sales:
1-800-456-6798 or business@simonandschuster.com

Manufactured in the United States of America

10 9 8 7 6 5 4 3 2 1

Library of Congress Cataloging-in-Publication Data is available.

ISBN-13: 978-0-7432-9735-6
ISBN-10:   0-7432-9735-0

Dedication

THERE was a time when my grandmother Alice Black was a young, strong, fiery woman who raised a family on her own. She was tough, spirited, and proud. I grew up watching the struggles and adversity she endured. From her I learned to be strong and to never compromise my principles. Although she suffered from a hard life, she never quit or let people get the best of her. She was a fighter and would sacrifice or do anything for her family.

I loved and admired her growing up; I still do today. However, it breaks my heart to see what Alzheimer's disease has done to this remarkable woman. She can't speak anymore or remember very much. Most of the time she doesn't recognize me or her children. The few smiles the last couple of years that I have gotten from her, and the love in her eyes that she has been able to give, have meant everything to me. I am powerless to help her remember. It hurts me to my core that I can't save the woman who saved me. While I can't make her remember, I can honor her, and that is what I try to do. It is her spirit that is in my blood, that gives me the heart to take on all the criticism and never yield. I am many things, and I have made my share of mistakes, but one thing no one can ever accuse me of doing is backing down. I have stood my ground and fought for what I thought was right. No one can deny that. Most of all, I am Alice Black's proud grandson who will always love, cherish, and respect everything she has taught me. She deserves that!

—T.O.

To Casie:

Thank you for inspiring me to be a writer. You gave me the confidence and desire I needed to take on this project and see it through. I love you. I tell you that every day, but this time it's different. This time it's published for the world to read. I tried my best to make you proud, as I do every day!

—J.R.

Acknowledgments

As for my family, their support was there when I needed it most. We all hung in there together like a family should. Grandma would be proud of the way we stuck together and stayed strong. I couldn't be more proud of my mother, Marilyn; my sisters Tasha and Sharmaine; and my brother, Victor.

I would like to thank Felisha Terrell for inspiring me to want to be a better person. She has brought me a lot of happiness in an otherwise tough year. I look forward to happier times with you.

Kim Etheredge has been more than a publicist, she has been a true friend. She has been there for me through all the tough times. This may be hard to believe, but I have, on occasion, been a bit difficult to deal with; nevertheless, she knows, no matter what, she is part of my family.

I knew when I first met Drew that it was fate, and now we've made history. We were in the foxhole together, took on unprecedented attacks, and won the battle. Thank you for negotiating the contract I dreamed of, and for helping me get control over my life. Sorry about the April Fool's joke.

I would like to thank Jerry Jones, Bill Parcells, and Stephen Jones for believing in me.

Jason Rosenhaus doesn't get much hype, but he proved to be a great coauthor on this book and a great coagent in my NFL negotiations. Having been there with me firsthand, I knew he was the right man for the job.

My attorneys Richard Berthelsen, Jeff Kessler, David Faher, Adam Kaiser, and David Greenspan went to bat for me at the arbitration hearing. I appreciate the hard work they put into it. We may have lost the arbitration case, but we won the war with the new NFL Collective Bargaining Agreement that brought justice to the NFL and helped me become a Dallas Cowboy.

My "dream team" deserves thanks for taking care of my off-the-field affairs: Jeff Rubin, Robert Bailey, Allan Lerner, Ed Rappaport, Peggy Lee, Daniel Martoe, Matt Cassano, Mike McIntyre, Pat Harris, and Erick Carter.

Last year, Philadelphia Eagles wide receiver coach David Culley was in a tough position being between me and management, but he always was supportive and never sold me out.

The Philadelphia Eagles' training staff was outstanding, especially trainer Rick Burkholder, who was a special guy to me last year. Thank you for being honest and, most of all, for being a friend that I trust. When the pressure was on, you stood by me. I won't forget it.

In addition to Rick, Dr. Hank Sloan, Mike Hatrack, James "Buddy" Prim, Brian Glotzbach, and Carol McMakin all gave their best efforts to help me rehabilitate my injuries in time to play in the Super Bowl.

My literary agent, Ian Kleinert, and Bob Bender of Simon & Schuster.

My friend and bodyguard Carlos "Pablo" Cosby for literally watching my back.

Pastor Anthony "Rev" Gardner for his wise and Godly counsel.

I appreciate my teammates who had my back and stood up for me when it wasn't easy. There are a lot of players I would like to thank, but I want to specifically mention Jeremiah Trotter, Correll Burkhalter, Todd Pinkston, and Justin Jenkins.

—Terrell Owens

I want to thank Terrell for having the confidence in my talent and the trust in my character to be his coauthor. I appreciate the patience he showed to make sure we got it in his words, and that we got it right.

I want to thank Kim Etheredge, Terrell's publicist, who has been the guardian angel for Terrell. Her tireless and unselfish dedication to her client is truly remarkable. You have been a blessing to Terrell with his career and this book. If there is such a title as co-coauthor, you deserve it and much more. Terrell was extremely lucky and smart the moment he hired you to be his publicist and lifesaver.

I want to thank Richard Berthelsen, Troy Vincent, Mark Levin, Doug Finniff, Tom DePaso, Patricia Shyu, and Todd Flanagan of the NFL Players Association for their direct and indirect assistance with many facets of this project.

I want to thank one guy who doesn't get a lot of recognition but who everybody loves—Robert Bailey. And the new kid on the block—Danny Martoe—for his help as well.

Finally, I want to thank Drew—my brother, my partner, and my best friend. Thanks for working overtime (as if you weren't already) to cover for me. We are what brothers are supposed to be!

—Jason Rosenhaus

Contents

Introduction

I wrote this book for a lot of reasons, but the most important reason was that I wanted to communicate directly with you—the fan. So much of what I said and did was portrayed to you by the media. When I did a TV interview, you saw the edited version of what I had to say, rather than the whole interview. When I talked to reporters, they took the catchy, controversial lines and presented them as if that were all I had to say. When I did something on the field or on the sidelines, my actions were described to you by commentators who put their own spin on it. When the Eagles released a statement about my conduct, it was done only from their perspective. Yet, since the start of the 2005 season, I have not publicly responded to what was said about me.

Without knowing all the facts, the media have speculated about what happened behind closed doors, based on half-truths that were leaked to accomplish the agenda of anonymous sources. I wanted to respond to set the record straight, but I knew, as was the case with the apology I made on my front lawn, that the media would criticize one aspect or another of it.

Then, when the arbitrator upheld my season-long suspension—a decision that violated the NFL Collective Bargaining

Agreement—I knew I wasn't going to get a fair shake. The arbitrator's decision was such an injustice that it led the NFL to agree to change the Collective Bargaining Agreement so that no other player can ever again be punished the way I was. Even after that, I didn't complain. I kept quiet—until now.

How could I accept such injustice? By knowing that the day would come when I would be free of everyone else's control. It was a long road between the time of my suspension and ultimate free agency, but I made the journey.

This book—the process of writing it, of telling my story—helped get me there. These are my words, straight from me to you. My critics will be negative and try to tell you that I just lent my name to someone else's work, but don't be fooled. When they criticize me for telling you about the wild rollercoaster ride, the ups and downs, it won't mean a thing because this is my story and no one can tell you different. This was the only way I could communicate with you, one on one, without anyone else's interference. That was why, instead of a well-known writer, I wanted one of my agents, Jason Rosenhaus, to coauthor this book, so that I wouldn't have to deal with someone who wanted to put their own take on things.

I took on a world of criticism and hardship during my suspension. There was a great deal of uncertainty, and speculation that my career was in jeopardy. There were times when things looked extremely bleak. It would have been easy to give in to the negativity, but I refused. I had faith in God and myself that everything would work out. I disregarded the naysayers and pressed on. And it is my sincere hope that, if you happen to be down on your luck and the times are tough, maybe this book will help you keep the faith so that you can come out on top as well.

What I went through, all the craziness that happened, has been misportrayed to the public. Everyone else's point of view was out there, but not mine. Now, I'm telling my story like it really went down, regardless of the consequences. That is how I was raised to be.

So get ready to read about what it's like to be inside an NFL huddle, to be in the Philadelphia Eagles' locker room, to step onto the football field, to suffer and overcome a brutal injury, to rehabilitate against all odds, and to play in a Super Bowl. And that was the good year!

Get out your popcorn and be right there with me as I take you back to what happened with the wildest, most documented story of all from the NFL's last two years.

Make no mistake; this is not an apology or a defense. This is an explanation. I don't claim to be perfect and I admit I made my share of mistakes, but there is another side to the story that you haven't seen until now. I'm not asking you to love me, and I certainly don't want you to hate me. I'm just asking you to take into account what I have to say with an open mind. I want you to judge me for yourself, not based on what the media says, but based on what I have written in my story. Enjoy . . .

1
Yesterday's Loser

SCRAWNY and quiet—that's what I was like growing up in Alexander ("Alex") City, Alabama. Alex City is a small country town where there's nothing to do but get into trouble. As a teenager, I was the perfect target for the big bully on the block: I was skinny, awkward-looking, and kept to myself. The one thing I could do well was run, and believe me, I needed to do a lot of that. In my neighborhood, there was always a group of bad teens hanging out, waiting to pounce on a kid like me. They would stand on a corner and look for a loner walking down the street. After getting chased down and beaten up a couple of times, I became a good runner. Joining the track team in junior high school wasn't for fun, it was for survival.

I find it funny that so many people assume I was a star jock coming out of high school. They assume I was the most popular kid in class who got all the girls. I wish! That couldn't be farther from the truth.

They think I have a loud, self-promoting, fast-talking personality. They could not be more wrong. I'm actually a pretty quiet, straight-up country boy—until you cross the line. Once you cross that line, you're gonna hear from me and there ain't no going back. What that line is, well, that depends.

One afternoon while I was in high school, I was riding home on a school bus after a track event. I made the mistake of falling asleep on the bus. It was just my luck that the biggest and meanest kid in school was on that bus, too. I was physically exhausted and passed out in a deep sleep. I was breathing through my mouth and it was open as I slept. The jerk came over and hocked up a big wad from his throat and nasal passages. He dropped that huge, disgusting gob of spit right into my mouth.

I slept right through the whole thing while everybody laughed at me. I didn't find out about it until later. Can you imagine the shame, the humiliation I felt when I went home and told my family? For what seemed like an eternity, I was teased and tormented unmercifully by the kids at school. I had been a loner before that happened, and became even more isolated after.

Everyone laughed at me. I tried to block out the image of his spit entering my mouth, but I felt nauseated every time I thought about it. Knowing that he disgraced me and got the best of me was more than I could handle. From that day on, I was done being a pushover. Yesterday's loser was determined to become tomorrow's winner.

A couple of days later, a bigger, older kid caught me walking by myself. He was looking for trouble, and I had a big target on my back. I was supposed to be his entertainment for the day. As soon as I turned the corner, I saw him running after me. I reacted by doing what was natural for me—I ran. Then I remembered something my grandma told me.

She said, "If one of those big bullies tries to get you, pick something up, hit him with it, and run."

And that's just what I did. I stopped, grabbed a brick, and turned to face him. I was tired of being the loser in these fights. I'd had enough of getting bested. I was ready to stand up for myself. I felt overcome by a wave of emotion, a rush of adrenaline, and I felt the strength of God in me. He saw my face, the brick in my hand, looked at me again, and ran away.

Then a funny thing happened: I started chasing him. I ran after him with that brick and tried to beat him down with it. The whole thing looked like one of those Tom and Jerry cartoons where they take turns chasing each other. I laugh about it now, but it was terrifying at the time.

Eventually, we got near my house and I stopped chasing him. As I walked through the front door, still holding that brick, I felt something new—satisfaction. When I got home and told my grandma and mom what I had done, they laughed. I laughed, too, and then I saw that they were proud of me for standing my ground. All of a sudden I found a sense of pride.

After that day, I could never again go back to being the wimpy coward who was the butt of everyone's jokes. The problem was that I couldn't walk around with a brick in my hand everywhere I went. The other thing on my mind was that I was tired of being too skinny to do this and too weak to do that. My football coach never put me in to play because I was just a stick with oversized pads on that didn't fit. I couldn't fill out my uniform, so whenever I ran, everything wobbled. I was a joke and I wanted to be more than that.

I was raised in an extremely strict household where I didn't watch much TV and I just kept to myself. I remember one afternoon, when I was a young teen, and the Big Red chewing gum commercial came on TV. It was the one where the chorus is singing, "So kiss a little longer . . . make it last a little longer . . ." while they show couples kissing. It is certainly not R-rated, but my grandma acted like it was a XXX movie clip. Feeling that the commercial was inappropriate for kids, she got angry and turned that TV off for the entire night.

. . .

I spent my days staring out the window, alone with my thoughts. After sitting in my room long enough, the answer to all my problems came to me. I realized it was time to get acquainted with my high-school gym.

I started lifting weights. I had all the motivation in the world to get bigger, stronger, tougher, and faster. I worked out in the high-school gym every day, whenever the school and my mother would let me. All I wanted to do was pump iron. It was hard work, but I didn't care. The physical pain replaced the mental pain and I liked that. Pretty soon I started to see a change. Muscles started developing and strengthening. My biceps, abs, chest, and quadriceps started bulging. I could feel myself growing stronger and running faster. The more progress I made, the harder I worked. I emerged from that summer with a sense of purpose and entered my senior year of high school as a different person, physically and mentally.

Although my body matured, the feelings of shame and failure were only a memory away. Eventually the other kids forgot about the spitting incident and I made a couple of friends along the way.

Feeling a little more confident, coordinated, and cool, I decided one afternoon in my senior year to go to the record store and hang out there with a friend of mine. The shopkeeper sold records, tapes, candy, soda, clothing, and just about anything else kids would want to buy. It was a cool place to go after school and had become a popular scene in the projects.

For once during my extremely rigid and isolated upbringing, I was having a good time. Then trouble walked in the door. One of the other players on the football team came looking deliberately for me. A few days earlier, the head coach had asked me about an incident that had taken place. As I was raised to do, I told the coach the truth about what happened.

The player didn't like it and came there to fight me. As I said before, I wasn't much into fighting, but it was going down and I had no choice.

When he saw that I wasn't going to back down, he threw the first punch and we went at it. I fought him toe to toe. Things got crazy in that store as his friend started fighting my friend. My friend and I fought our way out of there. I stood my ground, and he never messed with me again.

Not much has changed since. I still won't let anyone bully me. Whether it's over respect or a $49-million NFL contract, I'm going to fight for what I think is right. What no one in the media seems to recognize is that I am not about money. I am about the principle of what's right and wrong. When I'm wronged, I'm going to stand up and try to make things right. And because of that, I was crucified by the media and penalized more harshly than any player in the history of the NFL.

I made my share of mistakes, but I never broke the law or hurt anybody. My penalty was a four-game suspension without pay and being sent home the remainder of the season. An arbitrator ruled that it was appropriate that I be fined approximately eight hundred thousand dollars for my "disruptive" behavior. But what did I do? Did I murder someone? Did I rape someone? Did I hit someone with my car? Did I get arrested for a DUI? Did I get arrested for drugs? Did I use steroids? Did I beat on my wife? Did I abuse an animal? Did I hold out of training camp or any preseason games? Did I cheat? Did I hurt another player with a cheap shot? Did I quit on my team? Did I give a losing effort in the Super Bowl? Did I make racist or prejudiced comments? Did I use profanity? Did I lie? No. If I had, that would be okay. The NFL, the fans, and the media would forgive that. What no one forgives—is reality. The truth hurts. I spoke the truth. I bucked the system, said what I wanted to say, and took on the NFL. That was my crime. For that, the bully came after me harder than anyone before.

The media have portrayed me as the bad guy because I am not politically correct and will not be a "company man."

When I was a young player in this league, my idol, the great Jerry Rice, told me, "TO, at some point you're going to have to learn to be politically correct. You know, give in, give 'em what they want."

As much as I respected him then and still do now, I told him, "Nah, not me."

I know my life would be so much easier if I could compromise my principles and say things publicly that I don't mean, just to appease people who don't care about me. I know I would have made more money. I know I wouldn't be taking so much criticism from the media. I know all of this. But I also know that the day I give in, the day I compromise, the day I stop being the ultracompetitor I am, is the day I won't be able to play this game anymore. I wouldn't be where I am today if I could be politically correct instead of honest. I can only be one way—my way. I am Alice Black's grandson and Marilyn Owens's boy! I have a simple code I follow that was ingrained in my soul by my grandmother and mother. That code demands that I be my best. That means being honest, working hard, and always doing what I think is right. Their spirit is in me. It's what drives me to go jump up and snatch that ball out of the air to score touchdowns. That spirit pushes me to beat the defender trying to stop me. If I compromise my spirit, I'll become broken and won't be special anymore.

For these reasons, I believe that I am the best wide receiver in the game today. I was not born this way. In high school, I was too skinny to get on the field. Once I got more muscular, as a kid growing up in Alabama, I dreamed about playing football for Alabama University, but the Crimson Tide didn't want me. The University of Tennessee at Chattanooga offered me a scholarship but was much more interested in our high school's other receiver. The NFL drafted eighty-eight players before I was picked, including eleven other receivers.

The year before drafting me, the 49ers traded two first-round picks to draft J. J. Stokes as the heir apparent to Jerry Rice. I was looked at as just another guy, nothing special. All my life, I have had to overcome adversity. How does a kid go from not being good enough in high school, to a backup receiver at a small college nobody knows about, to a Pro Bowl wide receiver with more than one hundred career NFL touchdowns? By having a big enough heart that through sheer force of will he keeps on beating the odds.

I am as good as I am because God has blessed me with talent and because I have worked as hard as any person on the planet to get here. Unlike so many other professional athletes, I eat with extreme discipline, rarely drink alcohol, don't smoke, and don't use illegal drugs of any kind. I sleep properly, lift weights, run until I drop, practice intensely, and do everything else humanly possible to be the best that I can be. No one can say that I don't train hard, practice hard, or play hard. I have overcome the pain of taking dozens of long needle injections all over my body including in my groin.

I have endured an enormous amount of bitter criticism in learning to accept that people have the right to express their opinions. I accept that fact and respect others, but that doesn't mean I believe everything they say. There are a lot of haters out there hoping I fail. Despite their negativity and enjoyment of my struggles, I refuse to stay discouraged and I will always press on. This past year I faced a great deal of uncertainty. There were tough times, but throughout it all I stood tall with my chin up and my head held high.

Why? I am a God-fearing man. I find my strength from my faith in God and my family. I believe that He has a purpose for me and isn't finished with me yet.

T.O.

I've heard in church, "You must go through the storm before you receive your blessings."

I have suffered through broken bones, torn ligaments, agonizing losses, unfair punishment, and extreme frustration—all for the dream of becoming a Super Bowl champion. I only know how to compete like a champion. That's why I can't give people what they want, because what they really want is to see me fail. I won't let that happen, and I'll fight with everything I have to stand up for myself until they knock me down and I can't get up anymore. You want me to compromise? Make me!

2

The Road to Free Agency

As a rookie, your first goal is to make the team. Once a player makes the team, at that point, he wants to become a starter, win football games, be invited to the Pro Bowl, and ultimately win a Super Bowl. Those are the dreams of football players. And as professionals trying to make enough money to support our families for generations to come, we NFL players have another dream. That dream is to become a free agent.

Free agency is the process by which a player who's made it through four seasons in the NFL has the right to negotiate with all thirty-two teams, determine a fair market value, and get paid what he's worth. It took a strike by the NFL players and years of hard negotiating by the NFL Players Association (NFLPA) to let players become free agents. The way the NFL works, until you have completed your fourth season, the team that you play for controls your rights. Furthermore, even after your fourth year, the team can designate one player as their franchise player and restrict that player from going on the open market. Don't get me wrong—the system is not perfect, but it works. The NFLPA has done an excellent job of providing free agency for veterans; I am living proof of that.

Although free agency can be elusive, if you stay healthy through four seasons and are a good football player, it's there for the taking. Some situations are more complicated than others. Unfortunately, my situation has been as complicated as it gets.

I was drafted by the San Francisco 49ers in the third round of the 1996 NFL draft. I went from the University of Tennessee at Chattanooga to a team that had won five Super Bowls under Joe Montana and Steve Young. I had never won a championship at any level. I was going to be catching passes from Steve Young and running routes with the all-time great Jerry Rice. I signed a three-year contract worth an average of $280,000 per year and dreamed of winning a Super Bowl with those two as my teammates.

The 49ers' coaches knew I had potential, but I was green and had zero technique. I was fortunate—although it didn't seem that way at the time—to have an excellent cornerback, Marquez Pope, to practice against.

Marquez was very physical and tough. He started out as a cornerback but was moved to safety because of his physical toughness. The coaches made him jam me at the line of scrimmage. Marquez didn't just jam me, he humiliated me. Here he was, a master technician, very strong and physical, and there I was, also strong but with no technique whatsoever. He kept pushing me and pushing me, keeping me from getting off the line. He was mean and nasty, but always in a positive way. He challenged and demanded that I learn how to fight back. Before long, the student became the master.

I became excellent at fighting off the jam and exploding past the defender. One technique I excel at now is the rip technique. This technique is good for when a defender comes in close and tries to push me with both hands. What I do is slap his hands away with my left hand and simultaneously rip my right arm upward from my hip to my head while running by him. The purpose of the upward rip with my arm is to simultaneously knock his hands away from me and create the momentum to stride forward, accelerating past the defender.

Little receivers try to move their feet quickly to run around a defender who's trying to jam them. I can move my feet like a quick speedster, but I can also use my power to plow right through somebody. I eventually learned different moves that I can use to counter every technique they throw at me. Marquez Pope taught me well.

So did Jerry Rice. One of the things that made him so special was his ability to anticipate the snap count and get off the line faster than any player in the history of the game. He shot out of his stance quicker than anyone and was impossible to cover one on one.

I was like a sponge, soaking up whatever information I could from him. One of the things I learned from him was the importance of a quick start, so I created my own technique. I liken it to a downhill skier who uses his poles to push off and get started. At the snap, I shoot my hands down as if I am pushing off the poles and explode past the defender.

The last touch in my development as a route runner came when my 49er coaches told me to use my basketball skills and envision myself on a basketball court playing one on one. They told me to pretend that I have the ball and have to get around the defender to get to the basket. All of a sudden it all came together and I began to advance from someone who wasn't sure he'd make the team to a guy who could play and contribute.

My rookie year, I was quiet on and off the field. I showed that I was good enough to play in the NFL, but I wasn't considered a starter. My second year, the 1997 season, Jerry Rice blew out his knee when he was tackled by Warren Sapp on a reverse. Due to Jerry's injury, I was thrown into the starting lineup and I played well, catching sixty passes for 930 yards and eight touchdowns. It was my third season, in 1998, that was the big breakout year for me.

One game in particular had the biggest impact on my career. We were playing the Green Bay Packers in early January

1999. I'd played well that season, proving to be a good starting wide receiver. Playing opposite Jerry Rice, I caught sixty-seven passes from Steve Young for 1,097 yards, and scored fourteen touchdowns during the regular season. But this was a playoff game. I was a good, but not yet great, player. And the way the game started out I was awful.

Steve Young was on fire that game, wanting badly to beat Brett Favre's Packers. Although Steve was playing very well, we were losing in the first half 20–17, and it was because of me. I dropped a lot of balls that day. The very first pass I dropped was going to be a touchdown. When the ball left Steve's hands, its trajectory sent it up past the stadium seats, into the sky, into the winter sun, and it came down fast. I lost sight of the ball until it was too late, and I dropped it.

On another drive in the first quarter, I fumbled the ball away. Steve kept throwing to me, but I was dropping pass after pass. At halftime on TV, the announcers were criticizing my play, repeatedly saying I was hurting the team with my poor play. And they were right.

To make matters worse, I dropped another pass from Steve Young on third down in the third quarter. I can't tell you how bad this felt. My mom, my grandma, and all my friends were watching me struggle out there. I hated letting them and my teammates down. I was so angry with myself that I became frustrated. I knew that if we lost this game, I would have to spend the entire off-season knowing I was the reason we were sent home. I was desperate to do anything to try to win the game.

I stood on the sidelines quietly with my arms crossed. I couldn't look my teammates in the eye. I thought about how the local San Francisco newspaper had a hero for every 49er win and a goat for every 49er loss. I knew the writers were penciling me in to be the goat. I didn't want my mother's son to be the goat for the next eight months.

The 49ers safety Marquez Pope came over to me and told

me to keep my head up. I heard him and appreciated it, but I was too frustrated to respond. I told myself that this was the playoffs, what I had dreamed of, that there was no time to be depressed.

As we got the ball back late in the fourth quarter, we were winning 23–20 with just a few minutes to go. This was our chance to drive the ball, kill the clock, put some points on the board, and prevent the Packers from getting back on the field.

As I put on my helmet, I told myself to catch the ball like my wide receiver coach Larry Kirksey told me—to watch the ball into my hands and not to look away until I had control of the ball. Receivers have a tendency to look away early, to see where the defensive back is and where the hit is coming from. I had made that mistake earlier and that was why I had dropped so many passes. This time, I was going to make myself look at the ball all the way.

We just needed a couple of first downs to run down the clock and win the game. When third down came, Steve once more went to me. I knew it was coming and I ran a great route, getting open. He threw a perfect spiral right into my hands. I made sure to watch the ball go into my hands. I did everything right and I somehow *still* dropped the ball. I rolled around on the ground and looked at my hands in disbelief. The replay showed me mess up again on national TV and the big screen in the stadium. I couldn't believe it. Now we had to punt the ball away. We had to give the ball back to Brett Favre and stop him from scoring.

I prayed the Packers wouldn't score and we would win. If we won, then we would have another game to play and I could have a chance to redeem myself. If we lost, it would be awful. I couldn't stand the thought of my mother's feeling the pain of her son's being the loser who cost the team the game and a chance at a Super Bowl. It was unbearable to think my mom would suffer because of what I did. I play this game for her and my family. I wanted to be successful so she could live in a nice house and we could afford to provide my grandma with the best possible care to treat Alzheimer's disease. My spirit comes from them and drives me to make their lives better, not worse.

It was agonizing to stand helplessly on the sideline and watch the Packers march down the field and score a touchdown. The Packers took the lead, 27–23, with less than two minutes to go.

We got the ball back on our own twenty-four yard line with 1:50 to go. Steve threw pass after pass, driving the ball down to the Packers twenty-five yard line with about fifteen seconds to go. I ran hard on every route and got open, but Steve threw the ball to Jerry Rice, J. J. Stokes, and the other guys. I couldn't blame him for losing confidence in me. On second and three, Steve called the all go double comeback play in the huddle. The play was designed for two receivers on the outside to run straight into the end zone by the sidelines, and for two other receivers to slant inside toward the middle of the end zone. I ran the play and I was open for a touchdown, but Steve threw to J. J. Stokes instead, even though Stokes wasn't open. The pass was nearly intercepted, and with eight seconds to go we had our last chance to win. This was to be the final play of the game.

Steve called the same play again. The whole world thought the ball was going to go to Jerry Rice, but I wanted the ball to come to me. No one would suspect that Steve would even look my way. When I got to the huddle, Steve looked at me when he called the play and I knew what he was thinking. As I took my stance at the line of scrimmage, I thought of doing it for my team. All that I wanted in the world was to catch that ball and to prove I could play this game. I prayed for that chance.

Steve yelled in what seemed like slow motion to hike the ball, and then I ran with strength and speed like I never had before. I was crying in my heart to get open. I was hungry for Steve to throw me that ball.

As I ran like a madman, I cut inside and exploded away, separating from the defender. I turned and saw Steve put the ball in the air. The ball soared right toward me, coming hard and fast in a perfect spiral. I wanted that ball like I never wanted anything in my life. No one was going to stop me. As I jumped up for it, I could see nothing but the ball, while the two defenders were coming to take my head off from both sides. They could have been armed with baseball bats and I was still going to get that ball. I watched my hands pounce on the leather and I could feel the laces. I clutched it in my hands with every ounce of strength I had and pulled the ball into my chest, bracing for the hit. They battered me with their best shots and we all violently collided at the one yard line. No matter what, they couldn't stop me. My determination pushed me through and kept my momentum going forward as I fell into the end zone.

I made the catch! I scored! We won! Game over! I cried tears of joy as my teammates hoisted me in the air.

"That was for you, Mom and Grandma! That was for you!" I cried. That was one of the happiest days of my life. That game changed my career. That one play turned me into a hero set on a path toward stardom. One play can really mean that much. This game is very unforgiving, and all it takes is one play to haunt a player for the remainder of his career. At the same time, one catch can make a player into a hero forever. This business is all about what have you done lately, and that's why one play from one big game can be all it takes to land a big contract. I gained a tremendous amount of confidence in myself and I knew deep down now that I was a winner!

We lost the next game, but my three-year rookie contract expired and I was a 49er hero. I had exceeded everyone's expectations and was penciled in to be the heir apparent to Jerry Rice. I was looking forward to getting rewarded with a fair contract.

To me, a fair contract is one that pays me what I'm worth. What am I worth? I'm worth what other teams would pay me for my services—just as an NFL team is worth what any billionaire is willing to pay, and an NFL TV contract is worth what any TV network will pay. I wanted the chance to earn what I was worth. Unfortunately, I did not get that chance.

To prevent other teams from making me an offer, the 49ers designated me as their franchise player by making me a one-year offer for $1.47 million. I was disappointed about getting franchised, because that enabled the team to make that one-year offer rather than a possible multimillion-dollar signing bonus and a long-term contract. The franchise tag meant the 49ers could restrict me from going on the free agent market and hitting the jackpot. Here I was, thinking that they would treat me right, that I was the future, and rather than let me test the market, they were able to keep me from getting a fair market value contract.

It was not that $1.47 million was not a lot of money. It was. The problem was that I was being prevented from making several times that amount. I was being underpaid for the value of my services. I didn't think that was right.

Throughout that fourth season, I just assumed they would do right by me and it would be a smooth negotiation. I thought that my agent at the time, David Joseph, would be able to easily negotiate a great contract for me. This is what a young, naïve player thinks. It doesn't take long for the NFL to teach its players the hard way that this is a business.

Before I knew it, the 49ers were sending us a below-market offer, and our head coach Steve "Mooch" Mariucci was publicly criticizing my agent. Mooch took a shot at David, stating that he had never done a big contract before and didn't know what he was doing. In hindsight, he may have been right. Regardless, this was my first taste of how teams use the media to sell fans their point of view.

Things got ugly. The negotiations turned acrimonious and I couldn't understand why. Eventually, though, after a couple of months, we came to an agreement on a seven-year contract worth nearly $35 million. The key to the deal was an initial signing bonus of $7.5 million, and that I could void out the remaining two years of the contract after the fifth year. That way, I could become a free agent in March 2004 while I was still young enough to command a top contract. This was crucial to me. Careers are short in the NFL. You have a very brief window of time to capitalize on your abilities before age and injuries start to slow you down. And, yes, seven figures is a lot of money—but I ask you, if you knew you could make a lot more money than you're currently making for doing the same thing, wouldn't you try to get it so as to secure your family's financial future? Of course you would. If I was able to beat the odds and somehow last five more seasons in a dangerous game, I wanted the chance to reach for another big contract.

And the thing to remember is, NFL contracts aren't guaranteed. If the 49ers decided along the way that I wasn't worth what they'd agreed to pay me, they had the option to cancel my contract, and to try to get me for less. Teams do this all the time, and players have no choice but to accept it or go elsewhere. Fans don't realize this, and the media don't report it much, either.

The seven-year contract wasn't what I could have gotten on the free market, but I figured it wasn't bad for a kid who was once a scrawny nobody not good enough to play high-school football.

.   .   .

From there, I began to flourish as a wide receiver. My confidence grew and I developed a natural feel for getting open, eluding tacklers, and scoring touchdowns. Unfortunately, while I rose to the top ranks of my profession, the team fell apart around me. Steve Young's career came to an end after the third game of that next season in 1999, and Jeff Garcia became my quarterback. The Niners were 4–12 in 1999, and it was a few more years before we got back to the playoffs.

During the 2000 season, I got my first real taste of controversy. My celebrating drew some serious attention when the Niners played in Dallas. I scored a touchdown in the second quarter, and then I ran from the end zone over toward the middle of the field and stood on the famous blue Dallas star, the symbol of "America's team." I raised my arms and looked up to the sky. My teammates loved it—and the Cowboys hated it.

Little did I know how significant that day would be.

When I went over to my bench, my teammates were patting me on the back for it. The Cowboys players, not surprisingly, responded. Dallas running back Emmitt Smith scored a touchdown later and emulated me, scolding the 49ers sideline. Throughout all the drama, none of my coaches or anyone else said to me that what I did was wrong, so when I scored once more in the fourth quarter, I did the same thing.

After the game, I was widely criticized and made out to be a villain. Look, I was trying to pump up my team—we were 0–3 and facing the Cowboys on the road. I got ripped by the media and felt for the first time the hypocrisy of many sportswriters. They criticize players for being dull and lacking personality, but then as soon as you let your personality come through they smack you down for it. I know their job is to sell papers, and I honestly respect that, but I felt a lot of what was said about me was unfair, and when I pointed this out, the writers got even more angry. If you want to criticize me, okay, but then I've got the right to criticize and call you out, too. The media outrage over my actions was loud enough that the 49ers' management suspended me without pay for one game, costing me $24,294. I didn't like the fact that my team caved in to the league instead of supporting its players. I don't think that's how things should be, not when we're the ones leaving our sweat and blood out there on the field.

One of the main stories of the 2000 season, as we finished 6–10, was Jerry Rice's 49ers career coming to an end. It wasn't that Jerry didn't want to play anymore, or that he was no longer effective—he played all sixteen games and caught seventy-five passes—but the Niners had decided it was time for a change, and he eventually signed on with Oakland and played across the bay for the next three-plus seasons.

Jerry's last game in a San Francisco uniform was at home against the Chicago Bears. The stage was all set for him to have a great game and go out in style, but the Bears were expecting us to try to force the ball to Jerry, and instead I caught a record twenty passes for 283 yards. They sent my jersey to the Pro Football Hall of Fame in Canton, Ohio, and I was named to the Pro Bowl for the first time.

In 2002, I was again in the middle of another media storm. On *Monday Night Football* against the Seattle Seahawks, I scored a touchdown. A friend of mine was at the game, sitting in the front row of the end zone. I'd promised him that if I scored a touchdown, I would give him the ball. That was the plan—until another idea came to me in the middle of the third quarter. Before stepping onto the field, I asked a team trainer to hand me a Sharpie. I put the marker in my sock and ran on the field. As fate would have it, I scored the winning touchdown, pulled out the Sharpie, signed the ball, and gave it to my friend.

All hell broke loose over this little celebration. I figured it was creative, and was not that big a deal. But Seattle's head coach, Mike Holmgren, thought differently and said to the media, "It's shameful. It's a dishonor to everyone who has ever played the game."

What? Give me a break! ESPN put me on the cover of its magazine, with a line that said it all: "Guys are beating their wives, getting DUIs and doing drugs, and I get national attention for a SHARPIE?"

At the end of the 2002 season, the 49ers fired Mooch and hired Dennis Erickson. The off-season going into the 2003 season meant a new start for me. After that season, I'd have the right to void the remaining years of my contract and become a free agent. I hoped to get a new deal done with the 49ers before the season started; my agent, David Joseph, met with them but they never actually made an offer. They stopped returning his phone calls and said they didn't want to negotiate until after the season. I was disappointed but remained determined to have a great year and help the team win a championship.

Unfortunately, in the 2003 season we went 7–9 and failed to make the playoffs. I had another Pro Bowl year, my fourth in a row. Despite wanting to play on a winning team, I was still willing to stay with the 49ers. With the season over, I had the choice of voiding my contract and becoming a free agent or playing out my existing contract with salaries of $5.3 million in 2004, $5.9 million in 2005, and $6.5 million in 2006. I had three years remaining on my contract because in 2000 I renegotiated my contract to add another year. After thinking it over, I decided to enter the open market, confident I could do better.

I was fired up. I had played eight years in this league and was finally going to become a free agent. I dreamed about going to a team that was just one wide receiver away from being a Super Bowl contender. I wanted to play for a team that had a quarterback like Steve Young. I was super excited to let the teams come to me so I could get a fair market value contract and play with a winner again. I couldn't wait!

3
The SNAFU

UNDER the terms of my contract, in order to void the remaining years and become a free agent on March 3, 2004, all I had to do was send a letter to the 49ers to let them know that was what I'd decided.

The contract stated that I had to send the letter by the last day of the 2003 season, which was technically March 2, 2004. My agent, David Joseph, explained to me that we had to send in the letter by March 2 for me to be available to all thirty-two NFL teams at the start of free agency.

So in mid-February, David flew to my house in Atlanta and we signed the letter allowing me to become a free agent. About a week after I signed the letter, David faxed it to the 49ers front office, at three in the afternoon on Wednesday, February 25.

That night, I was in a hotel room in Hollywood, California, looking out over the balcony at the big "Hollywood" sign. I had just ordered some Chinese food and overheard the TV in the background tuned to ESPN. My phone rang, but I didn't pick it up in time before it disconnected. I looked at the number and saw that it was David. Then, in the background, I heard an ESPN commentator say that Terrell Owens should fire his agent for negligence.

"What?" I went over to the TV and listened to the commentator say that I had missed the deadline to file for free agency. He said that I was stuck with the 49ers.

"That can't be, it's not March 3 yet," I thought to myself.

Then the phone rang again and it was David. I listened in shock and disbelief as David frantically explained to me that the NFL and the NFLPA had modified the Collective Bargaining Agreement. The new agreement had the effect of moving up the deadline in my contract from March 2 to February 21. David pleaded with me that he had no idea the date had been moved up because the NFLPA never told him, faxed him, or mailed him notice. The NFLPA was adamant that they had provided all agents with notice, including David. Regardless, we missed the deadline. We would not have missed it if he had sent the letter when I originally signed it.

Gene Upshaw, the head of the NFLPA, said to the *New York Times,* "We faxed the notice to TO's agent on February 10. We have confirmation of the note. We faxed pages. Now he claims he wasn't notified. I'm not going to sit around and take the blame for a mistake he made."

Whether it was David's fault or the NFL Players Association's fault, my free agency was botched. I did not know what to believe, who to trust, or what to do.

David told me that the NFLPA never sent him the fax on February 10 to notify him of the rule change. He told me it wasn't his fault. David was very negative toward the NFLPA with me. He told me they screwed up, not him. He told me not to listen to them and insisted they never sent the fax.

The NFLPA told me they knew for a fact that the fax was sent and received by David's office. They asked me if I wanted to file a grievance against him.

When I talked with David about the situation, he begged me to stay with him and promised me that we would appeal it and everything would work out. David was my agent for eight years. From the beginning of my career, he was handling my NFL contract negotiations, my marketing, my taxes, and my investments. I trusted him. I believed in him. He handled everything for me. How could I file a grievance against my best friend? What was I going to do—take money out of David's pocket?

I made a decision based on friendship, not business. I figured I would stick with him and see this thing through.

What it came down to was that I viewed David as my friend. Throughout my career, I wanted David to take the journey with me from the small time to the big time. I wanted us to be an unbeatable team.

I wanted all these things for the both of us, and now it all blew up in my face. I was in agony as I realized that the 49ers could take my free agency away from me. None of this would have happened if David was on the same page with the NFLPA or if he had just faxed the letter when I originally signed it. I could not believe that this could happen to me. My leverage in free agency was at stake, which could mean millions of dollars to me.

I could do nothing but watch the beginning of free agency come and go. Eventually, the 49ers told us to take a couple of days to try to work out a trade with another team. David had been talking to the Baltimore Ravens and the Philadelphia Eagles. The Ravens were not offering us close to what the Eagles were, plus the Eagles had the better quarterback, so we wanted to do a deal with the Eagles.

The situation got even worse when, without telling us, the 49ers traded me to the Ravens while we were negotiating with the Eagles. Neither the 49ers nor the Ravens told us about the trade until after they did it. David got into a verbal confrontation with the Ravens' management. David told me they'd insulted him, and when they called me, I took up for him and wouldn't talk to them.

The only positive was that the NFLPA filed a grievance against the San Francisco 49ers on my behalf to try to break the trade to Baltimore and make me a free agent. The NFLPA told me that there was a good chance that we would win and I would become a free agent, although it would be after the teams went out and spent their available money under the salary cap.

When Gene Upshaw called me, I was very standoffish and confrontational. Because of David's comments, I had come to look at the NFLPA as my enemy instead of my ally. I didn't realize that the NFLPA had spent a lot of money to hire Dewey, Ballantine, P.A., an outstanding law firm, to represent me in my challenge to the 49ers' claim that I was still under contract. I've since come to appreciate how much the NFLPA tried to do right by me.

It turned out that the NFLPA presented a tremendous case, and as the hearing got underway, the 49ers and Ravens knew they were going to lose. Before the special master could rule in my favor, the teams acted quickly, and the Eagles brokered a deal with the 49ers and the Ravens to send me to Philly. The contract the Eagles proposed for me had a guaranteed signing bonus of $2.3 million plus a roster bonus of $6.2 million, so that my first-year bonus would be $8.5 million, with a 2004 salary of $660,000. The second year had a salary of $3,250,000. The compensation over two years totaled $12,410,000. The total value over the length of the seven-year contract was approximately $49 million. But out of that $49 million, only the signing bonus of $2.3 million was guaranteed.

When the trade to the Eagles was taking place and David was negotiating the deal, I had changed my cell-phone number. David could not reach me. He cut the deal with the Eagles without me knowing all the details. When he finally reached me, he swore to me that he got every nickel he could from the Eagles.

A few weeks earlier, the Eagles had just paid free agent defensive end Jevon Kearse a $12-million guaranteed signing bonus plus a $4-million roster bonus, so that Jevon's first-year bonus was $16 million. Jevon's two-year compensation was close to $20 million and he had $12 million guaranteed. So over the first two years, Jevon's contract compensated him close to $20 million versus my $12 million, and his guaranteed money was $12 million compared to my $2 million. I was coming off a Pro Bowl year—several of them, in fact—and he wasn't. Who was his agent?

What was the real difference? Jevon was a free agent and I wasn't!

But David told me this was the best deal we could get and urged me to jump on it. He presented the deal as a winning solution to the situation we were in. He persuaded me that it was the greatest thing since sliced bread. I believed him.

So when the NFL Players Association was not in favor of us taking the deal, I sided with David, not with them. The NFLPA knew that the special master (Stephen Burbank) on the case was going to rule in my favor and declare me a free agent. That's why the 49ers and Ravens were all of a sudden willing to trade me to Philly. David's relationship with the NFLPA had become antagonistic and there was bad blood there, so I didn't listen to the NFLPA. I listened to my friend, my confidant for the last eight years, who fought to persuade me to take the deal. The NFLPA wanted me to follow through with the legal process to become a free agent. After talking with David, I had concerns that maybe we would lose my case. I had come to view the situation as the NFLPA versus David, not me versus the 49ers. It never occurred to me that perhaps David was trying to cover his own butt and get me to do the Eagles deal before there would be any negligence issues. Although the ideal situation would be for the special master to set me free, I decided to trust David's advice. Although David pressured me to go against the NFLPA, in the end, I am the one who's accountable, and the final decision was mine.

Once I made the move, I decided not to look back and focused on the positives. The Eagles were a team that kept making it to the NFC Championship Game but couldn't make the jump to the Super Bowl. I thought I could be the missing piece to the puzzle. I was excited to be an Eagle and to see if I could take that team to the Promised Land of Super Bowl Championships.

I decided to put the whole botched free agency episode behind me. I headed to Philadelphia with plans to soar like an Eagle!

4
Philly's New Favorite Son

ARRIVED in style: The Eagles flew me in on a private jet and sent a limousine to the airport to bring me to the team's facility. The fans were waiting for me to show up and greeted me like a big shot. I knew how hungry the fans were for a Super Bowl win after losing in the NFC Championship Game three years in a row. It was a very exciting time.

I worked hard that off-season leading up to training camp in late July. As the first game of the season approached, everybody had high expectations for me, no one more so than I. Not even head coach Andy Reid.

Right before the first practice, I was running around in a pair of black tights that I always wore in San Francisco. Practicing in tights was something I learned from Jerry Rice. I wanted to continue that tradition. On some men they might look pretty embarrassing. On me, they look good. In either case, they can be revealing.

Maybe that's why Coach Reid had a rule that any player who wore tights must also wear shorts. For eight straight years I had trained in tights without shorts. All of a sudden, I had to wear shorts with them and it felt uncomfortable. Nevertheless, I abided by his rules. However, I proposed a deal to him: I asked Coach Reid if I could wear the tights without shorts in the future if I scored fifteen touchdowns this season. He responded by not only saying yes, but saying that if I scored fifteen touchdowns *he* would wear the tights without the shorts.

Now Coach Reid is not known for his slender waist and handsome physique. No one is going to confuse his build with mine. Seeing Andy Reid walking around at practice in a pair of tights would be the funniest sight ever!

I set the mark at fifteen because I wanted to challenge myself. In 2003, the year before I got there, Eagles quarterback Donovan McNabb threw sixteen touchdowns for the whole season, and all of their receivers combined had fewer than fifteen touchdowns. I'd hit the fifteen-touchdown mark just once, when I had sixteen in 2001. In 2003, I scored just nine touchdowns. I knew it would be tough, but I believed in myself and had confidence that I could do it.

Not that I needed any more motivation, but I got pretty fired up for that opener at home against the archrival New York Giants. I'll never forget waiting in the tunnel for the announcer to call my name. As I heard the players called before me and watched them run out onto the field between the two rows of our teammates, I got emotional. I listened to the roar of the crowd, saw a sea of green 81 jerseys, and I thought of my family and of what I'd gone through to get to this point with this team. I was so happy to get a fresh start, to have a new home with a new stadium, new fans, and new teammates. I had tears in my eyes. When they called my name I was so charged up I ran through the tunnel at the speed of lightning.

Donovan saw those tears. We looked at each other, slapped hands, and said, "Let's do it!" We were both talking about the Super Bowl, and it all started with that game against the Giants.

The Giants scored first, taking the lead 7–0. After the Giants scored, I was determined to take over. We moved the ball down the field and approached their twenty yard line. Coach Reid called the play to go to me.

When I get excited and line up in my stance awaiting the snap, I wiggle my fingers rapidly. This doesn't necessarily mean the ball is being thrown to me; my fingers get antsy on a running play in my direction, too, as I prepare myself to block the defensive back, or if I'm getting ready to block for another receiver on a passing play in my direction. This time the ball was coming to me and my fingers got anxious.

That one or two seconds before the ball is snapped can sometimes feel like a long time. Before the snap, I don't get overly excited or scared. I'm cool. I think about how many yards I need for a first down and how to break free for a touchdown. I'm all business, and I avoid talking trash with the defender lined up in front of me, focusing on how I'm going to beat that defender.

One of the more common techniques defenders use against me is to try to jam me at the line of scrimmage and interrupt my route. In a West Coast offense like the Eagles were playing (and like I'd learned in San Francisco, where it originated), the primary receiver needs to be open at a certain spot at a certain time if he wants the quarterback to throw him the ball. If the defender can get in my way and push me off my route, I won't be at the spot when my quarterback is looking for me, and he'll either get sacked or look to throw to someone else. My quarterback is counting on me to be there and I am counting on him to get the ball there where I can catch it. It's all about timing.

The defender's objective is to disrupt that timing. A defensive back is allowed to push me and have contact with me during the first five yards off the line of scrimmage. What my opponents would like to do is get in my face, press me at the line of scrimmage, and prevent me from getting past them.

What they would like to do and what they can do are two different things.

Any person on the planet who tries to jam me at the line is going to have a tough time. Whoever they are, if they try to jam me, they've got their work cut out for them. I'm not bragging, that's just the way it is. I'm six-four in my cleats and 226 pounds of pure muscle. How is a six-foot, 200-pound corner going to stop me? It ain't gonna happen that way.

Plan B is to try to cover me by backing up five to ten yards deep to try to shadow me. Don't let my size fool you; I'm as fast and quick as the little speedsters, and I'm stronger, taller, and more muscular than the bigger defensive backs. I've also been trained by the best receiver to ever play the game, Jerry Rice, and I've been blessed with great wide receiver coaches.

It also helps that I've learned to eat healthily and with discipline. I worked repeatedly, tirelessly to perfect my techniques of getting off the line and running routes. I trained for speed and lifted weights for power. I do countless abdominal exercises to strengthen my core and improve my explosiveness. I stretch for maximum flexibility. I do all of this the entire off-season to prepare myself for that moment when I'm standing at the line of scrimmage waiting for the center to snap the ball, to break through the defender's jam, to run past him, get open, catch the ball, break the tackle, and score the touchdown. That was and is my focus. That's what I do. That's why I am a cool cat when everyone else is tight.

So when Andy Reid called my number, I ran my route, Donovan threw a strike, and my first catch as an Eagle went for a twenty-yard touchdown. My second catch was a three-yard touchdown. I scored three touchdowns and we won the game easily, 31–17. By the end of the game, Coach Reid may have gotten a little nervous about the bet.

To start the season with three touchdowns against the Giants was special. Right away, Donovan and I sent a message that the Eagles were a force to reckon with. I told Donovan that we could break records together and make history.

I learned this game catching passes from Super Bowl champion Steve Young. Steve was an outstanding quarterback who threw great spirals. By the time I developed as a Pro Bowl receiver, Steve was winding down, and I didn't get the chance to play at a high level with him for long. I developed an appreciation for a talented quarterback, and I hoped that Donovan could be for me what Joe Montana and Steve Young were for Jerry Rice.

Back in February 2004, at the Pro Bowl, Donovan had pitched me on coming to Philly. Ray Lewis, the Pro Bowl linebacker for the Baltimore Ravens, tried to persuade me to join his team, too, and while I had much respect for Ray, he didn't play quarterback. Baltimore's quarterback was Kyle Boller, and I was completely unfamiliar with him.

Donovan, on the other hand, I was familiar with and I liked. The 2003 season wasn't Donovan's best, and after talking with him I felt he had something to prove. He had a strong arm and was mobile like Steve Young. I had hopes we could be a Hall of Fame duo.

After that first game, our success continued. We won the next several games in a row. Everything was really coming together. I was developing a good relationship with Donovan and considered him a friend. Every Monday night, I threw a party at my house to watch *Monday Night Football* with the guys and have a good time. Donovan made it regularly and was the life of the party. He is one of the most likeable guys I know and can really have a fun personality. I had a nice bar at my house and Donovan got behind the bar and served all the guys there. He called himself "Ivory the Bartender," and was not Donovan for the night. We all had a fun time and grew closer as a team.

The Eagles had traditionally been a powerhouse on defense, but with me and Donovan clicking together to get the offense right, we were poised to make a Super Bowl run.

As tough as we were, after winning the first five games convincingly, we had all we could handle against the Cleveland Browns on their home turf. We found ourselves in the fourth quarter with the game tied.

In practice all week, we'd worked on this one particular play called "Z Dagger and Go." The play calls for me to run a very precise route. It's a difficult route to run because it requires beating double coverage. It works very well when teams try to cover me man to man with a corner and then double me with a safety. The corner is supposed to cover me closely, staying in between me and the quarterback, so if I break to the left or the right or come back, he should be in position to knock the ball away. But the corner is in big trouble on that coverage if I fake short and go deep on him, so teams use a safety to stay over the top of me to make sure I don't get past the safety on a deep route. The idea is for the corner to stay between me and the quarterback, and for the safety to stay between me and the end zone. The defensive plan is to keep me sandwiched between the two defensive backs and shut me down.

The Z Dagger and Go is designed to take advantage of my talent in a way that lets me beat the double coverage. How? It works like this . . .

The route calls for me to run straight up the field for exactly fifteen yards. At that fifteen yard mark, the cornerback should be behind me (from my perspective) and the safety should be in front of me. At the fifteen yard mark, I cut three steps inside and sell both the corner and the safety on the idea that I'm going horizontally across the middle. My objective is to get them both to commit toward running full speed horizontally over the middle. Since I'm running faster than they are, they have to commit or I'd pull away from them.

Once they commit by planting their feet and moving their hips to run full speed horizontally, I make my move. While that safety is still ahead of me but has his full momentum going across the field, I break my route vertically and shoot up the field, slipping past him. This way, I beat the double coverage and I'm open for a touchdown down the sideline.

I love this play and enjoyed working on it in practice, giving the Eagle defenders fits. Donovan and I ran this play every day in practice that week leading up to the Browns game. When Coach Reid called the play, I knew it was coming to me.

At the snap of the ball, I ran up the field, cut inward, and then broke down the field. Just as we practiced it, I was wide open. Only Donovan didn't throw it to me. He was supposed to, he should have, the opportunity was there for the taking, but Donovan threw the ball to wide receiver Todd Pinkston for an incompletion.

I was surprised and disappointed, because that would have won the game. I'd already scored two touchdowns, so it wasn't that I was upset about a lack of stats on my end. I have no explanation for why it happened. There was no reason for Donovan not to throw it to me. Had he made that throw, I would have scored, and we would have won instead of being forced into overtime.

Although I was disappointed, I told myself it was just a freak incident, an unintentional mistake by my quarterback. I decided to leave it alone and not say anything, because I figured it was just a one-time deal.

Anyway, in the end we won in overtime, so I moved on and let all be good and well.

And everything was great. It was all coming together and we believed that the Super Bowl was there for the taking. As the season progressed, things just got better. In the first seven games, I scored nine touchdowns. I was playing at the top of my game. That seventh win and ninth touchdown came against Ray Lewis's Baltimore Ravens.

The victory over the Ravens was a hard-fought, hard-hitting, low-scoring game that we won 15–10. I caught a season-high eight balls for 101 yards. I scored our only touchdown, which won the game.

My touchdown celebration made a lot of waves when I imitated Ray Lewis's pregame routine. Ray does a dance step with a figurative clutching of the turf. He then huffs, puffs, and pounds on his chest. It is very distinctive, and it's Ray's signature move. I imitated the dance perfectly and my teammates got a big kick out of it.

Ray is considered the meanest, toughest linebacker on the field. I respect Ray, and get along with him well, but this was our stadium, and when I step on the field, I'm afraid of no one. It's never personal against my opponents, I just want to win. To be at my best, I have to fire myself and my teammates up. That's what I did, and if anyone is upset by it, that's too bad, but I'm gonna do what I gotta do.

After the game, Ray criticized me, saying I acted in a cowardly manner by imitating his dance. My head coach Andy Reid had a different take. Coach Reid said to the media after the game, "TO came up big on several occasions, but down there he was very big. That was a great play he made for a touchdown."

The bottom line is that we were 7–0. Unfortunately, while I had really taken the town of Philadelphia by storm, dark clouds were forming.

5

The Turning Point

AFTER winning two hard-fought games back to back, we had our toughest challenge yet coming up against the Pittsburgh Steelers. We were 7–0, they were 6–1. Like the Eagles, the Steelers were traditionally a hard-hitting defensive team. The challenge was to see how our high-flying Eagle offense would do against the blitzing Steeler defense. They had an unproven rookie quarterback in Ben Roethlisberger and we had Donovan, so I liked that matchup.

At the time, we were considered by many experts to be the two best teams in the NFL, and this was the big showdown. There were a lot of eyes on this game to see who would take the title as the hottest team in the league at the midpoint of the season.

With so much hype surrounding this game, one of my offensive coaches came to me and asked me to be very positive and supportive toward Donovan. He told me that Donovan can get nervous and tight in big games. If things got rough and Donovan got into a funk, he wanted me to be there for Donovan and help get him through it. I told the coach I would.

As the coach may have suspected, the game didn't go our way. We just didn't play well as a team. Although I had seven catches, it wasn't enough to get the offense going. As all of us do sometimes, Donovan had an off day, throwing no touchdowns and one interception and completing only fifteen passes for 109 yards. No big deal; every player, including the quarterback and the receivers, has an off day during the season. That's why no team has gone undefeated since the 1972 Miami Dolphins.

During the game, Donovan was pretty frustrated. Nothing was going right and we were struggling to move the chains. To win, I felt we needed each other to be on the same page, and as my coach suggested earlier, I approached Donovan on the sidelines. I yelled that we could still win this game and shouted words of encouragement. I was being 100 percent positive.

I was trying to help him break out of that slump and get hot. I was fired up and I tried to get him to feel my energy. I don't know if he was embarrassed, didn't want to be cheered up, or just wanted to be by himself, but as I was shouting to him, he got up and walked away. I didn't take it personally; I knew he was a very competitive person and must have wanted to be alone to collect his thoughts. He and everyone on that sideline knew I was trying to be supportive and did not berate him in any way.

Unfortunately, we were the only ones who knew what I was doing. All that anybody could see from the stands and on TV was me yelling at Donovan while he got up and walked away. I admit it looked like I was harassing him; the media had no audio, so they couldn't hear what I was saying. They ran with that clip and rushed to tell the world that I was being a bad guy, without knowing what was going on. I had blown up once before on the sideline when I was a 49er, so everybody assumed that I was jumping all over Donovan.

To this day, the public still thinks I was being a bad teammate because that's what they were told, no matter how unfair, inaccurate, and wrong this was. Sometimes being misunderstood comes with the territory. I knew what had happened, so did Donovan and my teammates, and I accepted the situation for what it was and moved on.

Losing 27–3 and suffering our first loss wasn't fun. Neither was the bad rap that I got for my display on the sideline, but in the NFL there is never time for anything but getting ready for the upcoming game.

That next game would be on *Monday Night Football* against our NFC East rival the Dallas Cowboys. The fact that it was on national television in prime time made it even bigger.

To promote the game, ABC and the Eagles wanted me to do a skit for *MNF* to start off the telecast with a bang (no pun intended). The Eagles' public relations director, Derrick Boyko, approached me and asked me if I wanted to do it. He told me that I was *MNF*'s first choice and it would be a great piece. I do hope to get into acting after my football career is over, so I agreed.

The skit started with me dressed in full uniform at my locker, when I turned and acted surprised to see the seductive character Edie played by Nicolette Sheridan in ABC's hit show *Desperate Housewives*. We were all alone in the locker room, just before I was supposed to run out onto the field.

I said, "Edie!"

She was standing there before me wearing nothing but a towel wrapped around her. With sexy background music playing, she was staring back at me and combing her wet hair. She smiled and said, "Hey there, Terrell."

"What are you doing here?" I asked.

"Um . . . my house burned down and I needed to take a long, hot shower. So where are you off to, looking so pretty?" she flirted.

I enthusiastically answered, "Baby, it's *Monday Night Football*. The game starts in ten minutes!"

She laughed, "You and your little games."

Stepping in closer and caressing my shoulder, she suggested, "I've got a game you can play."

Being stern, I told her, "Edie, this is major. We've got Parcells and the Cowboys and Donovan needs me!"

Staring down and puffing out her lower lip, playing it just right, she complained, "Oh, what about my needs, what about . . . Edie?"

Sticking to my guns, I scolded her: "Will you stop it, all of Philadelphia is counting on me."

She answered back, "Well I can't help myself," and exclaimed, "I love you, TO!"

I demanded, "Then how about you tell me what's buried underneath that pool?" (This was a big secret on *Desperate Housewives*.)

Looking all sad, she said, "You know I can't tell you that."

Walking off, I told her, "Then I got a game to play!"

"Terrell! Wait!" She stopped me.

With the camera taking an angle from the small of her back upward, she removed her towel. ABC showed her bare back on national TV, nothing more. The camera then showed her from the neck up, staring seductively at me.

I looked her over and smiled, saying, "Ah hell, the team is going to have to win this one without me."

She jumped into my arms and the camera switched shots to show two other costars of *Desperate Housewives* sitting on the couch watching the skit.

The brunette, Teri Hatcher, complained, "Oh my God! Who watches this trash? Sex, lies, betrayal . . ."

The blonde, Felicity Huffman, agreed, saying, "And that woman! She is so . . . desperate. Yuck!"

Hatcher's character laughed and said, "I know what we should watch."

She grabbed the remote and changed the channel. The

viewer heard the *MNF* music playing as they both shouted ABC's signature, "Are you ready for some football?"

Then ABC aired the game and we won big over the Cowboys, 49–21. I scored three touchdowns and had a season-high 134 yards on *MNF*. That gave me twelve touchdowns in the first nine games. I was on fire!

Guess what? Nobody cared about what I or the team accomplished. All the press wanted to talk about was the racy skit.

When we filmed it, I thought it would be funny, exciting, and entertaining. It was definitely fun! My teammates loved it and they all wanted to know if Nicolette Sheridan was really naked. She wasn't. She had on a pair of very short shorts and wore pasties over her otherwise bare breasts. Then they wanted to know if I really had sex with her. Of course not! I had a girlfriend at the time and Nicolette had her boyfriend with her on the set.

They asked me if she was hot. I told them that, yes, she was very attractive.

They joked around, asking me if I got aroused. Although she was hot, sexy, and talented at piquing my interest, I was trying to be professional and do a good job of acting. Although I didn't get aroused, I could have if that was the direction they wanted it to go; I would have answered the call of duty, but it wasn't that kind of script.

In all seriousness, I knew my girlfriend and family would be watching, and we kept everything whistle clean. Nicolette was extremely talented and professional. I appreciated her compliments as well as the director's. After the game, I still hadn't seen the sketch, but I said to the media, "I don't know how my acting skills were, but I can't play football forever, so I'm trying to work on the Hollywood thing."

One of the reporters asked me if I had ever watched *Desperate Housewives*. I answered, "I will now."

After the game the Eagles' owner, Jeff Lurie, said he had no problem with the pregame tease. "I loved it," Lurie said outside the locker room at Texas Stadium. "I thought it was great."

The next day, ABC got flooded with complaints, and certain NFL personnel criticized me, which was the last thing I expected for doing something that the network and my team asked me to do. Once the Eagles heard the complaints, they backtracked from their earlier support. Their statement read, "We appreciate that ABC has taken responsibility and has apologized. . . . It is normal for teams to cooperate with ABC in the development of an opening for its broadcast. After seeing the final piece, we wish it hadn't aired."

ABC Sports vice president Mark Mandel said in a statement, "We have heard from many of our viewers about last night's *MNF* opening segment, and we agree that the placement was inappropriate. We apologize."

I have to admit that I felt a little betrayed by the way the team left me hanging out to dry. Controversy was nothing new to me, and on the one hand, I can understand parents (or grandmas like my own) on the West Coast at six o'clock Pacific time being upset about their children seeing a woman drop her towel and jump into the arms of a football player. On the other hand, I was doing something the team asked me to do, and they should have made that clear to everybody. Also, to be perfectly honest, I can't help suspecting that many of those calls were from racists who were angry to see a pretty blonde woman throw herself at a black jock.

What was I going to do? Who would care? Who would listen? I knew the answer. People are going to complain about anything I do, and I have no choice but to take it on the chin and press on.

I won't say it was easy. It really stung to be insulted by so many people for my involvement in the *MNF* skit. On the other hand, I felt like the fans in Philadelphia were in my corner, especially since we were winning, so I didn't let it get to me. We won our next game, which was against another NFC East rival, the Washington Redskins, 28–6. I scored another touchdown, and through just ten games I was leading the league with thirteen TD receptions, which tied the franchise record.

We were 10–1, and I was taking the League by storm. Even the media were complimentary, mentioning me and Peyton Manning as the top MVP candidates for the 2004 season. They were saying I was the difference between this year's Super Bowl–bound team and last year's disappointment. I was the big story in Philadelphia.

Reporters had picked up the story about my bet with Andy Reid, and there were jokes all over the place about how I was a lock to get to the fifteen-touchdown mark, and how funny it was going to be to see Andy Reid wear tights to practice. Article after article reprinted Andy's words, "If he scores fifteen touchdowns, I'll wear tights."

When they asked me about it, I said, "There's no way he can get out of this."

When they asked Coach Reid about whether he would hold up his end of the bargain, he just smiled at them.

I told the media, "I'm not really concerned about that, to be honest. I think it'll be great for everyone else, but we'll have to see how Andy holds up his end of the bet."

I really was feeling good about everything. We had that presence about us that a team gets when it looks destined to go to the Super Bowl. I had become pretty good friends with Donovan and with some of the other wide receivers on the team, and I felt comfortable with where I was for the first time in years.

During that week of preparation for the Giants rematch, Coach Reid put in some plays specifically designed for me to get the ball and score. I was excited when he called one of them on our first drive in the game. We'd run the play successfully in practice. It's designed to create a mismatch that forces the defense into covering me one on one with the weaker of the two corners. I will win that battle every time.

Reading the defensive alignment, I saw that Coach Reid had created the single-coverage matchup we were looking for. Without double or triple coverage, I could tell that it was going to work. Coach Reid had the right call at the right time and we all knew it.

So when Donovan took the snap, my juices were flowing and I exploded off the line. Using my well-practiced technique, my strength, quickness, and speed, I made my move and got past the corner trying to cover me. Having beaten my man, I separated from him, streaking down the sideline and looking for the ball. I was all fired up that I was going to score my fourteenth touchdown and get us going right at the start. Then I turned and saw Donovan look away from me and throw a short, incomplete pass to our running back.

I couldn't believe it. Donovan had time to get the ball to me. He wasn't being overly pressured by the defensive line. He was not forced to get rid of the ball. I was the primary target for Donovan to throw to; the play was specially drawn up to go to me. I was wide open, running down the sideline. It was an easy throw for a touchdown. Instead of taking the lead, Donovan ignored me, he ignored Coach Reid's design, he ignored his responsibility, and he threw an incomplete pass to a secondary target.

A quarterback is supposed to go through his progressions and look for the primary target first. If that receiver's not open, then the quarterback is supposed to find the second target next. If that second target is covered, then he's supposed to find the third or fourth option. Going through this progression isn't easy; a lot of quarterbacks struggle at this and eyeball the first target way too long. The great ones are able to do it and do it quickly.

A quarterback shouldn't stare at his primary target too long because the defensive backs are trying to read the quarterback's eyes, to see where he's looking. By reading the quarterback, the defenders can anticipate where the quarterback is going to throw the ball and can get a jump in the right direction. That's what happens when a defender appears out of nowhere to intercept a pass intended for someone who was wide open when the ball was thrown. If the first wide receiver in the progression is open, the quarterback has to get the ball to him in a hurry before the defenders can read the quarterback's eyes. Donovan is very good at getting the ball to his first target quickly.

My point is that Donovan was not working through his progressions when he chose not to throw what would have been a touchdown to me. I was open, and he knew I would be, but he threw an incomplete pass elsewhere. We worked successfully on that play in practice and everything that was supposed to happen on that play happened in the game, but the throw went somewhere else anyway.

Something was wrong and I could feel it. I flashed back to the Cleveland Browns game where the same thing had happened. I knew this wasn't just a one-time, freak accident any more. The games are only sixty minutes and are not forgiving. You only get so many opportunities, and if you blow them, you lose. I was there to help this team win by scoring touchdowns and if there was a problem, I wanted to solve it.

After the play, as I walked back to the huddle, I told myself to relax, that Donovan would make things right. I wanted him to know that the next time Coach Reid called that play, I would be open and we could take advantage of the situation.

I was concerned, not mad. We missed an opportunity to

score, but that happens. This was not the end of the world. I stayed cool.

When I got back to the huddle, in a friendly way I said to Donovan, "I was open . . . Dude, you missed me."

In all fairness, there is pressure on the quarterback in the huddle to hurry up and get the guys focused on the incoming play. There is not a lot of time for discussion. On the other hand, feedback is important so we can get a better understanding of what's happening on the field. What I said to Donovan was not an unusual thing. I communicated the same way with Jeff and Steve.

I thought we had the same kind of relationship, where I could be straight up with him. I wanted to communicate with him so we'd be on the same page. I was in no way being disrespectful or unfriendly.

I thought he'd acknowledge that he made the wrong read and should have thrown me the ball. I thought he'd be angry with himself for missing me and not scoring the touchdown. I thought he would say what Jeff usually said after we misfired, "I'll get you next time. Be ready." I thought we were teammates, having each other's back. I never thought in a million years he would say, "Shut the fuck up!"

Wow! I could not believe he said that to me. All I said to him were those seven words, and that was how he treated me. No quarterback, or any other player, has the right to treat a teammate like that. That was wrong. I hadn't gone on and on. I hadn't challenged his leadership or authority in the huddle. I'd said what I had to say and that was that.

I felt like he had no right to talk to me that way. Maybe if I were some rookie talking trash while he was calling the play, then you could say something like that. To say it to a veteran like me, who wasn't speaking over him, was totally uncalled for. I was so shocked that I didn't know what to say. Here I was a nine-year veteran in the league, as accomplished as any player at any position, completely professional, and he spoke to me like that in the huddle in front of my teammates.

It's not like I hadn't spoken to him in the huddle before; it's not like I was doing something wrong or he was under extreme pressure at a critical time of the game on fourth down. Steve Young or Jeff Garcia certainly never spoke to me—or to anybody that I ever saw—like that.

Talking to a veteran teammate like that in the huddle without a damn good reason is something players just don't do. Don't get me wrong, it happens from time to time when a wide receiver is out of line, but I hadn't been.

When I got to the Eagles in 2004, Donovan was looking to improve on his 2003 season, in which he threw sixteen touchdowns, had eleven interceptions and a quarterback rating of 79.6. With me as his receiver, Donovan was putting up the numbers he had been wanting to achieve.

We were both in the running for MVP, along with Peyton Manning. The problem was that I was becoming the new favorite son of Philadelphia. The Eagles were no longer the Donovan McNabb show—he had a cohost. I was happy to share it with him.

After what happened on the play and in the huddle, I began to think that maybe he didn't want a cohost and maybe he didn't like me getting more attention. I told myself that maybe he was trying to spread the ball around. Why, though? What we were doing was working great for the team. We were winning, and that's the bottom line. I was happy to share the ball with the other guys, and I was happy to give Donovan due credit.

I was concerned that Donovan resented the fact that I was getting so much of the Philadelphia glory that used to be his. I wanted to believe that I was wrong. I wanted to believe that Donovan didn't throw me the ball as Coach Reid had called for because he made an honest mistake. I went back to the huddle believing that. We definitely had a problem, and that problem was that a quarterback who just accidentally screwed up doesn't act so defensive and disrespectful toward the guy the play was designed for, who was open for a touchdown, whom he chose not to throw to.

I have to admit, I was hurt. I could not just shrug it off. From the moment I got to Philly, I treated Donovan with the utmost respect at all times. Just a few days earlier, the media had tried to get me to gloat about being ahead of the pace to score fifteen touchdowns, but I wouldn't; I was relatively humble and gave credit to my teammates, especially Donovan. I said, "Coming in, even when I made Andy the bet saying I wanted to score fifteen touchdowns to start wearing my tights, I thought about it and said maybe I set the bar a little bit too high because I knew the nature of the offense. I knew [Coach Andy Reid] is a guy that spreads the ball out and [running back Brian] Westbrook was the guy last year that had the bulk of the touchdowns and when you look at the receivers they really didn't have that many. I really kind of challenged myself when I did that. I think at the same time Andy realized the type of player that I am [and] he's using me in this offense as a playmaker, and that's what I've always wanted—to utilize me as the player that I am and can be within a offense, especially with a guy like Donovan. My Thanksgiving came in March when I got to be with Donovan."

I don't know what more I could have said to be supportive of Donovan. I wasn't trying to steal Donovan's thunder; I was trying to make us a legendary tandem like Joe Montana and Jerry Rice. That was what I wanted for us, but in that instant in the huddle I knew he wasn't like Joe or Steve. They were positive, respectful, and encouraging in the huddle toward their receivers.

I admit I can be moody and difficult at times. I get emotional because I have such high expectations. I grew up that way, but I tried to be Donovan's friend. I wanted us to be close and tremendously successful together. But after I got so much hype following the *Monday Night Football* game, something was different. I tried hard to share the credit with him, but I guess it wasn't enough to maintain our friendship. For whatever reason, he wasn't the same guy toward me and some of my teammates noticed.

The only thing I could think of was that he disliked all the credit I was getting on his team. I had been Donovan's biggest fan. I believed we would be able to relate to each other and not turn on each other. He was a big part of my desire to go to Philly. He received a lot of unfair criticism calling him overrated. The tough thing was that as Donovan was finally putting together a season with big-time numbers, he was still overshadowed in the media by Peyton Manning and myself. Maybe he didn't feel that he was being recognized. Whatever it was, something was getting to him and he didn't look my way as much.

As for me, I did my best to stay focused after the insult in the huddle. I tried not to let what he said get the best of me and ruin my performance. The rest of that Giants game, I kept myself together and stayed professional. I was upset but I didn't let anyone notice, not yet, at least.

I thought about saying something, but we were on a roll. So I let it slide even though it ate me up inside. I knew eventually I had to say what I was feeling.

Donovan only threw four completions to me that game. The week before it was only two. I could not stick my head in the sand and pretend nothing was wrong. I had to talk to him and try to make things right.

After the game, I decided it was time to speak my mind. I knew if I approached him in front of a crowd it would get blown out of proportion, so I waited.

When the locker room cleared out, I went over to him. I

waited until after he was showered and dressed. There were still a couple of guys in the locker room, but the media were gone.

As I approached him, Donovan saw me and I could tell he felt awkward. I told him that I was coming to him man to man to let him know that I did not appreciate the way he spoke to me. I told him that he didn't talk to his other receivers and teammates like that, and I expected him to treat me the same way.

I didn't talk to him like I was scolding him; I talked to him like I was upset but respected him and wanted to work things out.

I really thought, after the way I handled things, that he would apologize and we would get back on track, but it didn't go down like that. There was a lot of tension in the air. He seemed shocked that I approached him, and he reacted by standing up to me. We stood face to face and it became confrontational. All Donovan had to do was apologize and we would have been cool, but he wouldn't do that. For whatever reason, he had a problem with me. In my mind, he had no legitimate reason or right to have any problems with me whatsoever.

This was crazy! Here I was standing toe to toe with a guy I considered my friend, who benefited from our relationship in a big way, acting like he wanted to fight. This was crazy! I couldn't believe it. I don't know what happened to my friend, but this wasn't the same Donovan I had cared about. What happened to the guy I hung out with in Hawaii at the Pro Bowl, who said he'd like me to join the team to win a Championship?

Whoever this new person was, he was not the guy I knew. When I think back on it now, though, I did know that person. He was that same bully that spat in my mouth. He was that same bully that chased me down the block until I picked up a brick to fight back. He was that same bully that attacked me in the store. I guess the more things change, the more they stay the same.

I never would have let things get violent and I don't think Donovan would have either, but running back Dorsey Levens still stepped in between us to settle things down. Trying to calm things down, Dorsey told us to talk about it on the bus.

I explained to Dorsey that I wasn't going to ride on the bus because I had already made plans to catch a ride with another teammate. I told Dorsey that I wasn't going to wait, that I wanted to settle this now.

Rather than be a team leader, be man enough to apologize or nip the situation in the bud, Donovan walked off to go do a postgame interview. He brushed off what I had to say and dismissed me as unimportant.

So much for my taking the initiative to talk to him like a man. All that did was make things worse.

When I was with the 49ers, I went through a strained relationship with my quarterback Jeff Garcia. I wanted to avoid that with Donovan. I bent over backward to avoid that negativity and ugliness. I wanted everything to go right with the Eagles where it went wrong with the 49ers. As I stood in the locker room watching Donovan walk off and throw away our friendship, I was devastated. I could see that Philadelphia was no Garden of Eden and that paradise was lost.

I could see that I was alone in a place where you can't trust anyone and have to watch your back. I've been there before; that's where I grew up. That's what I was used to. So I did what I always do; I picked my chin up and kept moving forward.

A couple of days later, Donovan gave me a call. Donovan told me that he was not ignoring me, but that he was trying to spread the ball around to the other guys, too. He let me know that things were going to be done his way, that this was his team. I could respect that; the quarterback is supposed to be the leader on the team, and it takes the whole team to win a game. However, he wasn't friendly or apologetic, but defensive. This was where our disconnection began. I felt like I was on the phone with a business associate, not a friend or a teammate I was close with.

Donovan was never the same with me again; things were only going to get worse.

6
From Bad to Worse

I **WANT** to make one thing clear: I was not angry because Donovan threw the ball to someone else and cost me a shot at glory. I am not a selfish player. When other receivers catch the ball, I take great pride in blocking defenders to help my teammates score. In fact, I was known for my blocking when I played with Jerry Rice. I'm a big, strong, physical receiver. I want to win and don't expect every pass to come to me. A pass thrown to someone else is no big deal. I'm happy whenever we score, whoever gets the touchdowns. It's when the team is losing that I get frustrated.

I was angry because the play was called for me, we practiced it during the week, he was supposed to throw it to me, I was open, and it would have been an easy touchdown. Even so, I could have gotten over that easily. That was not the reason Donovan and I fell out. Do not take this out of context and think that I got pissed off because he didn't throw me the ball when he was supposed to. That would be a terribly unfair and inaccurate conclusion.

I was angry because I went to talk to my quarterback as my team leader and my friend, and he completely shut me off, shut me down. He insulted me in front of my teammates in the huddle. That was a problem but I could have gotten over that, too, if he had discussed the issue. I still viewed Donovan as my friend even after he insulted me. He could have easily made things right between us, had he simply talked to me as a friend.

It bothered me that the person I thought was such a great guy turned out to be someone else. It made me angry that rather than seeing us as partners wanting to succeed together, he saw me as a competitor. It really tore me up that he could have very easily made things right and he didn't want to.

There are very few people whom I let into my personal life as friends. I wanted Donovan and me to be like family. And to be fair, up until that game, he was like family and a friend to me. But in the locker room after the game, when he walked away from me after I tried to talk to him and work things out, he turned his back on me.

So we were never close again and probably never will be.

I wasn't the only guy in that locker room who saw Donovan change toward me. Other teammates came over to me and said that Donovan didn't like my getting so much attention.

I don't expect any of my teammates to come out and publicly admit it. I wouldn't want them to. It's not their responsibility, and they should not get involved. But everyone in that locker room knew what was going on.

And the way things were, Donovan was under a spotlight that next game to see whether he was going to do the right thing and execute the plays as Coach Reid called them. We were at home playing the Green Bay Packers. With all eyes on him, Donovan did what he was supposed to do—he got me the ball. I caught eight passes for 161 yards and scored my fourteenth touchdown. I set the Eagles record for the most touchdowns in a single season. We won big and our record was 11–1. Although everything seemed rosy on the outside, the thorns were there.

With me having fourteen touchdowns, the media were in a frenzy. I was coming off a big performance and was ready to score that fifteenth touchdown. No one seemed to care that I broke the Eagles record for touchdown receptions in a single season; it was all about our hefty coach slipping into slender tights.

Donovan was quoted as saying, "That's nasty," when asked about it. I guess he didn't want to see that happen. That next game, with the pressure off him, he didn't throw me any touchdown passes but we still won. I just went about my business and kept my focus on the Super Bowl.

Up next for us was the Cowboys game. Our record was now 12–1. I had three games to get that touchdown and everybody was looking forward to it. Well . . . almost everybody.

The Cowboys were a rough and tough team. They had a fast, hard-hitting secondary. For reasons I could not explain, Donovan didn't throw my way much in the first half. Heading into the locker room at halftime, we were losing 7–6. I had one catch for four yards.

We were at home and the fans weren't happy. They came to see us put points on the board. All those 81 jerseys in the stands wanted to see me score that fifteenth touchdown to help win the game. The 67,723 fans weren't braving the cold December weather in Philly to see us losing to Dallas at the half and me with one catch for four yards. We were all frustrated.

When we got into the locker room, the coaches knew they had to get the ball to me in order to get the offense rolling. So when we came out to start the third quarter, Donovan's first pass went to me. The play was designed for me to run downfield and then come back to a spot twelve yards from the line of scrimmage. I ran my route and caught the ball. I was running across the middle of the field moving horizontally when I saw one of my teammates blocking a defender toward the sideline. Twenty yards downfield, I made a move to run around the block and the safety grabbed the back of the collar on my jersey and pulled me down from behind. That type of tackle, known as a horse-collar tackle, was made illegal after the season was over.

When I was grabbed by the collar, my momentum was carrying me toward the sideline. When he pulled me downward by the back of my shoulder pads, there was tremendous torque on my right leg. That leg had all of my weight and his put on it at an awkward angle. I heard a pop and felt searing pain shoot through my lower leg. The leg collapsed and I knew right away I was hurt. I immediately grabbed my ankle and thought the ligaments in my ankle were what had popped. Hoping I could walk it off, I somehow managed to stand up. My right foot felt dead. I couldn't move it. I forced myself to take a couple of steps and gingerly limped off the field.

The team trainer, Rick Burkholder, came running over to me. I had hurt my ankle before and played on a bad ankle sprain. I have a high threshold for pain, but I'd never felt anything like that before. The pain running up and down my leg was excruciating. I knew this was much more than an ankle sprain. I told Rick to take me straight to the locker room.

Once inside the locker room, we took an X-ray. I was relieved when the results showed that the bones in my foot and ankle were not broken. Fortunately, we won the game. Unfortunately, I knew that I was hurt very badly and my season was in jeopardy.

We scheduled an MRI for the next day, and I tried to stay optimistic. After the game, Coach Reid was asked about my injury. He said, "The positive is, it's not broken. The negative is, it did swell up."

When Donovan was asked about my injury and the possibility of its being serious, his response was, "We've been to the NFC championship without TO."

To be fair, a leader was supposed to say that the team would still be successful without me. The media tried to make Donovan's remarks seem negative, but I left it alone; I had bigger problems.

That night my ankle was killing me. It hurt so much that I couldn't sleep. I lay down on the couch and kept it elevated with ice on it. I remember I moved once to get up and lowered my leg; all of the blood came rushing down into my leg and the nerve endings shot fire through me. The severe pain told me I was in trouble, no matter what the X-ray had showed. I tried to keep a positive outlook and hoped the MRI results would be encouraging, but I had a bad feeling about it.

The next morning, my foot was even more swollen and the pain shot up all the way from my ankle to just below my knee. Lowering my foot again in the morning was agonizing. I walked on crutches with my foot in a special boot.

I reported to the Eagles' training facility at 8:30 A.M. to take the MRI. My leg was hurting pretty high up from the ankle, so they took the MRI of my entire lower leg.

The results showed I had an ankle sprain and a broken leg. For a more technical explanation, here's what Rick told the media:

> When the MRI came back, he did have a deltoid [side ankle] ligament sprain, which is what we saw all the bleeding from last night. . . . However, he does have a fracture of his fibula, about 10 centimeters below his knee. Anytime you see a sign like that, you see this fracture, what we call an oblique fracture so it kind of spirals up, we know that he had some unbelievable force at his ankle that transmitted up through his fibula and fractured it.

Once we got the results, the Eagles drove me to Maryland to see Dr. Mark Myerson, an ankle specialist. After looking at the MRI and examining my leg, the doctor told me I needed to have surgery as soon as possible.

Dr. Myerson told me that it takes ten weeks to come back from that type of injury. The Super Bowl was only six and a half weeks away. This was hard news to accept. I asked Rick if it was possible that I could be ready by then, and he said it was not impossible. Rick added that although I wouldn't be 100 percent, I had a remote chance of being recovered enough to play. I clung to that small hope, but I was really down.

During a conference call, I told the media, "I went down there optimistic, hoping for the best, and I got the worst of news. Things happen. You've just got to move on from it. . . . There's no reason for the city of Philadelphia to get down because I'm not there. . . . Obviously, my presence will be missed, but we have the guys to get it done . . . I was looking forward to the playoffs, really trying to get this team to the Super Bowl. I think without me, still, they can achieve that goal . . . I'm behind them. I'm going to be their biggest cheerleader."

My disappointment was evident from what I had to say. I was talking as if I had no chance of playing again this season. During my nine-year career, I only missed seven games, and now they were telling me I would be out ten weeks. The way they were talking, it looked like my season was over.

Rick's statement to the media explained the situation very clearly:

As soon as T.O. came back from MRI, we sent him down to Dr. [Mark] Myerson in Baltimore and that is when I reported to you this morning that we needed to do more testing. What they did testing-wise was they actually put T.O. to sleep just like for surgery and they externally rotated his ankle like what happened to him in the injury last night while he was asleep to see whether those bones widened.

They did widen, so he is going to need a surgery to repair that. He is going to need what is called a syndesmotic screw put through both bones in his ankle to stabilize that joint. That screw is pretty big. It goes through the fibula and the tibia and it stabilizes the joint. The fracture up high, the fracture that we saw ten centimeters below his knee, that is going to heal up on its own and that is not really the issue. When we saw that, we knew something else was going on in his ankle other than this deltoid sprain and so that was our red flag to get him into the hands of an ankle specialist.

Those ankle specialists, when they do the X-ray, they put them to sleep and they have to know just how much to turn that ankle so they don't do more damage. . . .

The obvious question from everybody is, what does this mean to his season? What does this mean to his career? Normally it takes a little longer for that to heal. You want the screw to sit in there long enough to stabilize the soft tissue.

At three weeks, we are going to test him out a little bit. We are going to put him on a bike, put him in the pool, let him run. If everything goes well in the surgery, at three weeks we will do that. We will send him back down to Dr. Myerson and let him check him.

If everything is going well and he is healing up, at five weeks there is a chance he can run. . . .

Seven weeks from yesterday is Super Bowl Sunday. If things would work out, there is an outside chance that he can be prepared to play in that game in some role. There are a lot of hurdles that have to be taken on before he can ever get to that point.

I had surgery the next day. Afterward, Dr. Myerson stated to the media, "While it is not unreasonable to hope he plays in six weeks, it's not something we would expect."

Rick was a little more optimistic in his statement. He said

that I stood "only an outside shot at being able to play in the [Super Bowl] on February 6—if [the Philadelphia Eagles] make it that far. . . . The scenario I painted is the best-case scenario, but it is realistic."

Rick explained that there was a "tremendous amount of damage" to the ankle and that if I didn't respond well to the rehabilitation, I would have to rest for three months before the screws came out in a second surgery.

To make things more complicated, I had injured that ankle before, which increased the medical risks of rushing back to play in the Super Bowl.

I had doubts. I found myself with a broken leg, with screws and a plate inserted into my ankle. I couldn't walk. The best-conditioned NFL athletes, guys younger than me who worked tirelessly day and night rehabbing their ankles, couldn't make it back in less than ten weeks. How the hell was I going to be ready to run routes and take hits in six and a half weeks?

How? The same way this too-skinny, too-wimpy, too-shy, not-good-enough-for-high-school-football, not-good-enough-for-college-football, nothing-special draft pick, just another guy in the League, became an NFL superstar!

How? Through my faith in God!

How? By believing with all my heart, body, and soul in Philippians 4:13: "I can do all things through Christ who strengthens me."

Before I got out of that hospital bed, my religious belief lifted my spirits. I left whatever doubts I had in that room. I might have had a broken leg, but I went back to Philadelphia determined to fly again!

I knew the odds were against me, that experts had doubts about me, but I took a positive attitude and went to work.

When I arrived back at the Eagles' facility, the media were waiting for me. I told them, "I feel I'm a pretty good healer, believe me. I've already moved my hyperbaric [oxygen] chamber down to my living room. I'll be in that, trying to get myself back on the field as soon as I can. I'm going to be smart about the situation."

This time my words weren't about my not being there; this time I was talking about making it back for the big game.

A lot of my teammates told me to go for it and encouraged me to believe that I could do it. They told me to be ready because they were going to make it through the rest of the season, win their playoff games, and go to the Super Bowl. They told me they needed me to help them win that big game. I knew that if I could play, it would be a huge lift to the team and really get their confidence high and their state of mind right.

The media seemed devastated that I wouldn't be around to give them something to write about. They seemed especially disappointed that I didn't make that fifteen-touchdown mark and force Coach Reid to put on the tights.

When they asked him about it, he said, "I made that very clear. The tights are on hold."

It seemed a lot of things were on hold. There were two games left in the regular season. We already had the best record in our conference by far and were assured of home-field advantage throughout the playoffs. We were guaranteed a bye week the first round of the playoffs and would only have to win two home playoff games to make it to the Super Bowl in Jacksonville. The problem was, the Eagles had lost in the NFC Championship Game at home the last two years to the Tampa Bay Buccaneers and the Carolina Panthers. Three years ago they'd lost on the road, to the St. Louis Rams. I hoped that if they did their part and got through those play-off games, I would be ready. So I went for it.

Rick had me rehabbing my leg immediately. Right away he got me in the pool to try to move the leg in a non-pressure-bearing environment. After a couple of days, I started to walk slowly and very lightly in the pool on a treadmill. Each day I walked with a little more stress on that leg. Each night, I spent hours upon hours sleeping in the oxygen chamber.

The hyperbaric chamber is the best investment I ever made. They cost around twenty thousand dollars, depending on the model and options. They work by increasing the oxygen in the blood flow. The high amounts of oxygen in the red blood cells help heal the damaged tissues. I was in that oxygen chamber for what seemed like all day every day. For the next month, I lived in the pool and in the oxygen chamber.

While working hard, I ate with extreme discipline on a very strict diet. I had blood work done to evaluate what amino acids and other nutrients my body needed more of, and custom-tailored my diet to maximize my health. I was taking twenty pills a day. Using the blood work analysis, my trainers formulated a special mix of amino acids I was given intravenously.

Since it was during the football season, I refrained from drinking alcohol, and I tried to get the proper amount of rest. If I wasn't in the pool or at the facility, I was in my oxygen chamber. I did everything they told me to do the best that I could. I can honestly say that I gave my best effort and could not have tried any harder. It wasn't easy, but I had fun doing it with that training staff.

The Eagles lost the remaining two games, but those were games in which the team had nothing to gain, since home field advantage was already locked up. Coach Reid did not play many starters for those two games, resting them for the playoffs. Still, it would have been easier to push myself through that grueling regimen if they had won those two games and looked like a lock to make it to the Super Bowl at Jacksonville.

A month after my injury, the Eagles had their first playoff

game, against the Vikings. By this point, I had progressed from walking in the pool to jogging in the pool to running in the pool on a treadmill. The trainers let me attempt to slowly and carefully jog on the field. I was unable to do so without a noticeable, painful limp. I still couldn't put much pressure on my leg or ankle. The crack in my fibula and my screwed-tight ankle joint were still very tender. With three weeks to go, I wasn't close. Although I was disheartened knowing I had a long way to go with a short time to get there, Rick was very encouraged and told me I had done better than he expected and that I still had a shot.

There was a lot of anxiety to deal with, but I kept to my faith and believed. I disregarded my doubts about being ready and rooted my team on to victory. The Eagles beat Minnesota, 27–14, and we were just one win away from going to the Super Bowl. As I watched them play, I had a feeling the Super Bowl was coming.

The next game, against the Atlanta Falcons, was for the NFC Championship. That game was life and death to me. I prayed for victory. The Eagles had lost in this game the last three years.

I was fired up when I stepped onto the field as the pregame introductions were underway. I felt empowered, being one Eagles win away from going to my first Super Bowl. Something moved me and I decided to jog on to the field. The fans went wild. I waved my towel and lifted my arms to salute the cheering crowd. It was a very uplifting moment for me.

I stood on the sideline, rooted for my teammates, and fired up the crowd as the Eagles won 27–10. I was very emotional that day, as everything I had worked for my entire life—to have the chance at becoming a Super Bowl champion—was happening before my very eyes.

When the game was over and it was official that we were

going to the Super Bowl, I left all doubt on the field as I walked off.

The next day at the Eagles' training facility, the media were waiting for me. They wanted to know what I was going to do. They wanted TO to make a bold statement. I did not disappoint them.

I said, "What a lot of people don't realize is that I've been doing a lot of rehab on my own, a lot of healing on my own, but spiritually God is healing me and I'm way ahead of where a lot of people expect me to be. . . . Spiritually I've been healed and I believe that I'll be out there on that field Sunday, regardless of what anyone says."

When the media asked Donovan about me, he said, "We can win it without TO. But, if he is there, we can win it with him and we are definitely going to try to win it without him."

People were a bit surprised Donovan downplayed my situation, but I wasn't. We weren't as close anymore and I didn't expect him to act like we were. I just became more determined to play, and that Monday I told the world that I believed I'd be able to do so.

Unfortunately, on Tuesday, January 25, when I visited Dr. Myerson, he disagreed. After examining my ankle and fibula, he told me that if I tried to play in the Super Bowl, I could end my career. The doctor explained that if I took a hard hit in my leg or ankle, or put too much pressure on it, I could break the screws and reinjure myself. If that were to happen, after all the trauma it had been through, the ankle might never recover well enough for me to play again. The risk to my ankle was career-threatening. To make matters worse, my fibula was still tender and could snap with a hard hit. That, too, would threaten my career. The danger was so extreme that Dr. Myerson refused to clear me to play.

Although he said I wasn't ready, he did clear me to run on a treadmill. He told me that even if I was at the point where I could run and change direction without pain, the ankle and fibula were still very vulnerable and would be susceptible to reinjury. That I could physically run and feel good wasn't enough. My bones and ligaments needed more time to heal, strengthen, and solidify. If I were to get injured, I would never be the same for the rest of my life.

As I listened to the top medical expert in the country tell me I couldn't do it, I felt a wave of stress hit me. I wanted so much for him to walk into that room and tell me that he had great news, that I was way ahead of schedule, that my body was healed, and that I would be medically fit to play. I would have given anything for him to say that to me. I wanted encouragement. I needed him to give me that green light to go for it.

When that didn't happen, I didn't get down. I refused to accept failure. I would not let him stop me. I believed that through my faith in God, I could do it.

I told him that I understood the risks and thanked him for doing a great job. I told him I appreciated everything he'd done for me but that God had cleared me to play. I didn't mean to come across as arrogant; my faith had gotten me that far, and I had to keep the faith if I was going to have any chance at all.

The challenge that Dr. Myerson put forth only made me more determined to succeed.

I drove home that night and ran on the treadmill as Dr. Myerson had cleared me to do. That was not encouraging either. I had a significant amount of pain in my ankle and fibula as I gently put the full pressure of running on it.

Thursday was the last day before the team was leaving town to start practicing in Jacksonville. If I was going to have any chance of being able to play, I knew I had to test myself that day by running on the field. Before that I had done some light jogging, so this was a big step.

The goal was to be able to run full speed without a limp. At first, as I gradually increased my speed, everything felt good. As soon as I tried to use a burst and accelerate, the pain kicked in. I tried to run through it, but I started limping. I wasn't limping badly, but it was just enough to alarm my trainers. That, too, didn't go as well as I had hoped. Regardless of the facts, I wasn't going to let reality ruin my dream. I went ahead and did my treatments on the leg, drove home, got into the oxygen chamber, and slept in it.

The next day I boarded the plane with the team and headed off to Jacksonville. From that Friday through Sunday, I worked around the clock with my trainers, Carol McMakin and Brian Glotzbach, NMT, as well as my chiropractor, Michael Hatrak, and his wife and daughter-in-law. Around the clock, Carol ran the electrical microcurrent through my ankle and my chiropractor massaged and aligned the tissues properly with my bones. I didn't really know the medical specifics of what they were doing, I just believed in them.

That weekend, as well as through the whole rehabilitation period, Rick Burkholder spent a tremendous amount of time on me. He worked tirelessly to help me and gave me everything he had. He deserves all the credit in the world for being not just an outstanding trainer, but also an outstanding person and friend. I grew to like Rick very much and always will. Rick was my main supporter from start to finish. I don't think I could have gotten that far without him. This guy was all class and nothing but loyal. His character is as good as it gets. With Rick in my corner, I felt like a confident, well-prepared fighter stepping into the ring.

When Monday arrived, it was a big day. It was the first day of team practice. I told my teammates, trainers, and coaches that I was going to participate and that was what I did. For the first time since I broke my leg, I was back practicing with the guys. I took part in fewer than one-third of the plays and limited myself. I ran full speed but didn't plant too hard on my right leg when I changed direction. I got through practice with no problems and for once my chances looked good.

After practice, my trainers worked on me relentlessly and I felt very encouraged—so much so that when Tuesday arrived, the big national media day of the Super Bowl, I walked out onto the field and took center stage.

I stepped onto the podium and everything came to a complete stop. All eyes, microphones, and cameras were on me. The cameras started rolling and I didn't leave them in suspense.

I looked out upon the hundred or so members of the media and told them, "I will play on Sunday."

I was up there fielding questions for an hour. At times I praised God for giving me the strength to get there. I told them God had brought me there for a reason, the reason being for me to play. I told the world, "If you don't believe in miracles, just wait until Sunday."

After practice, the guys were talking about how much fun they had been having going out and partying at night. After living like a hermit for the last six weeks, I decided to join them for a little while. It was a fun break, but I left the guys, went back to the hotel early, got into my oxygen chamber, and went to sleep. Every night I was there, I slept in my chamber.

The next day, I went all-out in practice. The screws and plate in my ankle restricted my range of motion and flexibility. I wasn't quite as explosive as usual. I tried participating in all the reps in practice but my fibula, more so than my ankle, started hurting pretty bad. It was a tough day and it was cold, around forty degrees or so, and raining. That cold rain was not exactly what I wanted to run around in. The pain was getting progressively worse with each repetition. By the middle of practice I was limping and they pulled me out.

More determined than ever, I went back to the hotel, got treatment, and went to bed early again in my oxygen chamber. Between meetings and curfew, the guys didn't have a whole lot of time to go out, but they made the most of what they did have.

With a ton of treatment and a good night's rest, I was surprised at how well my leg felt on Thursday. I thought it would be sore from the previous day and worse off, but it wasn't. I felt better—not great, but better. So after practice, I got treatment all night and another good night's rest.

Friday's practice was the key practice in preparation for the game on Sunday. I knew Coach Reid and the guys were watching me to see if I was finally ready to be in full form and I was. I had an excellent practice on Friday. I made it through without limping and had full speed. I felt strong. Sure, I was in some pain, but I have a high threshold for pain and could tolerate it. In the NFL, everybody has to play with pain and I take pride in being able to do so. I felt ready to go and thought I proved it in practice.

So the next day, on Saturday, I was really surprised when Coach Reid asked me if I was going to be ready. I could see he still wasn't convinced after the practices I had that I could withstand the full contact. I was disappointed he had his doubts. I looked him in the eyes and told him that I was going to play. I left no room for doubt. I made my point and told him that he could count on me to be there for him on Super Bowl Sunday.

I went to bed that night ready to wake up and show the world the impossible.

7

Super Bowl XXXIX

LEADING up to the game, there was talk that I was just talk. The media made numerous predictions that I would not be able to play. Some said that even if I did play, I wouldn't be strong enough, fast enough, agile enough, or conditioned enough to be a factor. They said I was going to be nothing more than a glorified decoy.

Worst of all, I read articles that accused me of being selfish for even trying to come back. Some people in the media stated that Andy Reid shouldn't let me play. They said that I was hurting the team.

Would they have said the same thing about Bret Favre if he were in my position? If you'll forgive my saying so, the effort I gave to rehabilitate my leg during that six-and-a-half-week period was nothing short of heroic. Through extreme effort, discipline, sacrifice, and faith in God I got myself ready in two-thirds the time that it takes all other professionally conditioned athletes to recover from the same surgery. I put my career at risk and went against medical advice to try to help my team win a Championship. Isn't that what old-school athletes are supposed to do? Was Curt Schilling being selfish when he pitched in the playoffs on his bloody ankle? Was Willis Reed selfish when he limped onto the court for the Knicks? For people to label me as selfish for trying to help win a Super Bowl Championship is terribly unfair.

My whole career people have expressed opinions of me that are ignorant, inaccurate, and insulting. I've come to realize that their hatred toward me is nothing more than jealousy. Someone once told me that strangers offer opinions; friends offer counsel. Knowing this, I refuse to let the haters out there hurt me. My faith in God shields me from all the arrows they shoot at me.

They don't hurt me. They help me. I take their dare and I challenge myself to win.

So to all my detractors I say, keep on criticizing me, it just motivates me to get better.

A decoy, huh? I don't think so! I went to bed with all this motivation on my mind, but when I woke up that Sunday morning, I felt relaxed. I prepared myself mentally as I would on any other game day. I guess the best way to describe my mindset would be to compare it to that of a boxer stepping into the ring. Some guys are all fired up and emotional, talking trash and making a show. Other guys have an intense, caged focus. There is rage in both, but the disciplined fighter has better control than the other guy. I am that disciplined fighter. Leading up to the game and during the live play, I am controlled and focused on the task at hand. I celebrate after the knockout, not before.

When I stepped into Alltel Stadium, I kept my emotions in check and stayed focused. I wanted to be calm and cool. I didn't want to overexert myself.

Inside, I had the attitude that I was a bad man, one you didn't cross. Too many people had taken their shots at me, and now the time for payback was fast approaching. On the outside, I looked intense and focused, but not overly emotional.

I got there a little early to get a feel for the aura surrounding the big game. I wanted to soak it all in and get accustomed to it. When I first went to the San Francisco 49ers, they were coming off five recent Super Bowl victories. As a rookie, I just assumed that I would get my share, too. I never thought it would take me nine years and a green uniform to get here.

Capturing the moment, I looked at the scoreboard, at the fans, and just absorbed the whole Super Bowl atmosphere. I went back into the locker room, suited up in my uniform, and came out onto the field again. This time I was all business as I ran routes full speed. I planted hard on my leg and tested it all out. I was running around and catching balls as if I had never been injured. While I was warming up, there were Patriot players videotaping me as I ran. Satisfied with how I felt, I went back inside and stayed relaxed.

After the pregame introductions and the nighttime fireworks, the game was finally underway. We took the opening kickoff and began on our thirty-nine yard line. On the second play of the drive, I caught a seven-yard pass. The reality that I had made the first reception in the Super Bowl hit me. Right off the bat, I showed I was no decoy. I sent a message that I was going to be a force all night long. It was intense, and I couldn't feel the pain anymore. In fact, I felt strong, like Superman again.

I was ready to drive the ball down the field and score. Unfortunately, on the very next play, Donovan got sacked for a loss of eleven yards and the referee ruled that he'd fumbled the ball away. Coach Reid made a smart move by challenging the referee's call. Upon instant replay review, the call was reversed, and we got the ball back and punted.

Our defense played an outstanding game. The Eagles defense under Coach Reid has been tremendous throughout the years and this day was no exception. The Patriot offense couldn't score, so they punted the ball back to us on our seven yard line.

Coach Reid ran it on first down, but we lost two yards. Then on second down and twelve Donovan threw me the ball, and I took it nine yards. Being deep in our own territory, Coach Reid made the safe call and ran it with running back Brian Westbrook on third down for two yards. We came up a yard short and had to punt.

Once more, our defense stopped the Patriots, and we got the ball back on our twenty-six. To get Donovan comfortable and in a rhythm, Coach Reid called for a bunch of short passing plays. Donovan started throwing short passes to Brian and to tight end L. J. Smith. They caught the ball just beyond the line of scrimmage and ran for a few yards after the catch. We nickel and dimed them a few yards at a time, but it worked. We got a couple of first downs and moved the ball to midfield.

The smart Patriot defense made adjustments to shut down the short pass and challenge Donovan to throw the ball up the field. On first down at the fifty yard line, Donovan tried once more to dunk the ball off to Brian, but they had it covered and tackled Brian for a three-yard gain. Donovan tried it again on second down but couldn't complete the pass to Brian. So now it was third and long, and a short pass wasn't going to get it done. The Patriots knew we had to go deep on them to get into scoring range, and they played off instead of tight.

Coach Reid called the perfect play. Taking advantage of the soft coverage, I ran a five-yard route across the middle and Donovan threw it to me. After catching it, I kicked into high gear, ran around the traffic in the middle, and bolted down the sideline for a thirty-yard gain. That was the big play we were looking for to get the offense going.

On that play, I showed the world that TO was back. I showed the world that I was healthy and the playmaker, the game-changer the Eagles fans needed me to be. I celebrated the moment on the sideline with a little dance, flapping my arms like an eagle.

At that point in the game, I didn't let the pain distract me. I wasn't scared that I was one hit away from ending my career. I believed so much that something special was going to happen that I was not afraid. I was confident that I was destined to have a great game.

To make things even better, there was an unnecessary roughness penalty against the defense on the play, which moved the ball to the eight-yard line. Yes! We were in position to score and take the lead. Then, on first down, Donovan got sacked for a loss of sixteen yards back to the twenty-four yard line. No problem, we still had two more downs and were within scoring range. On the next play, we went for it. I ran my route three yards deep into the end zone, but the Patriots intercepted the ball and returned it thirty-two yards to the twenty-nine yard line. Fortunately, there was a penalty for illegal contact on the play and the play was called back.

Okay, we got the ball back with a first and ten at the nineteen yard line. We were back in position to take over. On first down, Donovan dropped back and had all day. There was no pressure on him and he had all options available to him. Unfortunately, he stared down Brian and lofted a pass toward him near the end zone. The Patriots' strong safety read Donovan's eyes, broke on the ball, and intercepted the pass.

We wasted a huge opportunity in a game where opportunities can't be wasted.

At least the Patriots were backed up to their own three yard line. Once more, our defense delivered and forced the Patriots to punt. We got the ball back with great field position at the Patriot forty-five yard line. Our defense had played well, and it was our turn to carry our weight.

On first down, Donovan threw an incompletion to wide receiver Todd Pinkston. On second down, Donovan gave up a sack. On third and long, Donovan threw a short pass to our tight end but he fumbled it. Another missed chance for our offense.

Our defense sure didn't miss any chances. They stopped the Patriots three and out for the third time in a row as the second quarter started, and we got the ball back at our nineteen yard line. Trying to get Donovan comfortable, Coach Reid called for running plays and throws to Todd Pinkston. Since I was drawing double and triple coverage, it was easier for Donovan to hit the other guys. Coach Reid's strategy worked, Donovan got a big play on a forty-yard completion to Todd, and we finished the drive with a six-yard touchdown pass to L. J. Smith for a 7–0 lead.

The Patriots responded by driving the ball down the field to our fourteen yard line. Our defense responded by swarming Tom Brady and forcing a fumble, getting us the ball back with our lead intact.

After a couple of incomplete passes to Brian and to Freddie Mitchell, we came up short and had to punt. This time, the Patriot offense couldn't be stopped and they scored a touchdown. The game was tied with a minute to go in the first half.

We tried to move the ball into scoring position but the clock ran out on us at the half. Going into that locker room I had three catches for forty-six yards.

During halftime, the players formed into their groups by position and met with their position coaches. It was very organized and just like any other halftime. There was no great speech or anything like that from Coach Reid. It was business as usual.

The Patriots got the ball at the start of the third quarter and marched down the field to score another touchdown. They took the lead 14–7.

After a low-scoring first half, Coach Reid did what he usually does to get the offense going: He called my number. On the first play, Donovan threw me a pass that went for ten yards and a first down at midfield. That was a good start. The rest of the downs were not so good that drive. Donovan got sacked again and threw an incompletion toward another receiver. We had to punt the ball away. This time our defense held up and forced them to punt.

We knew we needed to do something with this drive or risk letting the Patriots pull away from us. So Coach Reid called for Donovan to throw the ball to me and for Brian to run the ball. Donovan completed two more passes to me for eight and seven yards. The offensive line played exceptionally well, opening holes for Brian and giving Donovan all day to throw. Brian took advantage of the good blocking and ran the ball effectively. Donovan capitalized by throwing Brian a ten-yard touchdown.

The game was tied at 14 with three minutes left in the third quarter. The Patriots responded by marching down the field sixty-six yards in ten plays to score a touchdown. They had the lead back with most of the fourth quarter still to play.

When we got the ball back, Donovan threw a couple of incomplete passes, Brian ran the ball for a loss, and we had to punt.

The Patriots moved the ball on us and kicked a field goal to increase the lead to 24–14. Down by ten points, we got the ball back on our twenty-six yard line with eight minutes left in the game. The first play went to Brian on a two-yard run. On second and long, we had to do something. With everything on the line, Coach Reid called my number.

I knew the ball was coming to me as I lined up toward the left sideline. My responsibility was to shake the cornerback and get open nine yards down the field. I knew Donovan was counting on me to be open at the right spot at the right time. The corner lined up right in front of me, thinking he was going to jam me and disrupt my route. At the snap, I moved my feet as if I were fighting to go outside toward the sideline. I faked going outside to the left and got him to commit to the left. As soon as he turned his hips toward the outside, he tried to push me and knock me out of my route. I slapped his hands away and cut inside on him. The moment I broke to the inside and separated from the defender, Donovan fired the ball in there.

As I caught the ball nine yards downfield, the defender had changed directions and lunged inside toward me. I spun around toward the outside and let him slip by me. I ran through the corner's outstretched arms and streaked down the sideline for a thirty-six-yard gain. Having moved the ball from our twenty-eight yard line to their thirty-six, we were back in the game. This was our chance to score a touchdown and narrow the deficit to only a field goal.

On the next play, Donovan dropped back, had good pass protection from the offensive line, and threw a wobbling duck that was picked off four yards beyond the line of scrimmage. Another interception, another squandered opportunity. At that point, things looked bleak for us. It would've been easy to give in to the doubt, but we were a team with a heart that wouldn't quit.

Even though the Patriots had the ball back and we were down by ten points with only seven minutes left, I still believed we could win. The defense gave us a chance; they stopped the Patriot offense and we got the ball back at our twenty-one with five minutes to go.

This was it. If we were going to have any chance to tie this game up, we had to score on this drive. There just wasn't enough time left to come back and put ten points on the board if we blew this one.

Coach Reid called two short passing plays, which took time off the clock and got us only eight yards. It was third down and we needed two yards. If we didn't convert here, the game was over. With the game on the line, Donovan came to me and I caught the ball for a first down. After two more ineffective plays, it was third down and eight. Once more, we had to have the first down. Once more Donovan went to me. And once more we got the first down, at our forty-six yard line, with 3:42 left. That should have been enough time, if we moved quickly, to score a touchdown, stop the Patriots, get the ball back, and move down the field to kick a game-tying field goal.

Donovan completed a couple of passes over the middle to move the ball to the thirty; however, we only ran two plays between the 3:30 and 2:30 marks. On the second play after the two-minute warning, Donovan threw a thirty-yard touchdown pass to a leaping Greg Lewis to bring us within three points with 1:55 left on the clock. As soon as we scored, I went over to Donovan. I congratulated him and told him that we were going to do it.

After an unsuccessful onside kick, the defense did all we could have asked of them, stopping the Patriots on three downs and forcing them to punt. We got the ball back, with forty-six seconds remaining, on our four yard line.

We had ninety-six yards to go in forty-six seconds. I believed with all my heart that we could do it. On the first play, Donovan threw a pass to Brian. We only got one yard and the clock ticked down twenty-four seconds to leave us with only twenty-two seconds left. We would have been better off if the pass had been dropped. On the next play, Donovan tried to go to me but we misfired. On third down, Donovan threw his third interception of the day and it was over.

I always thought we were destined to win that game. I fought through all the doubt and the skeptics who said I wouldn't be able to play. I showed my critics that I wasn't going to be just a decoy. I overcame all the odds and caught nine passes for 122 yards. I risked my career and the long-term health of my leg to win this game. My whole life I've wanted to win a Championship and we fell short. All of the spilled blood, the torn ligaments, the broken bones, the surgery, the injections, the brutal rehabbing, the countless torturous hours in the oxygen chamber—and we still ran out of time.

As the clock ticked down, the pain in my leg started to rise. We lost. That shouldn't have happened but it did. I was angry. I was emotional. I watched the Patriots celebrate and realized it had been a hard-fought game. The Eagles might have lost, but a lot of guys on our offense and defense played like winners. Walking off the field, I realized that I was one of those players. I stopped for a moment to look around and reflect on what I'd accomplished, what I'd proven, and what I showed the world; I felt proud. As an ultracompetitive person, I didn't like that we lost the game, but I accepted it like a man and moved on.

When the clock ran out, I congratulated some of the Patriots and then went into our locker room. I was in pain, but it was the kind of pain that reflects soreness rather than injury. I told Eagles trainer Rick Burkholder that I was okay, but he insisted that I get a quick X-ray to make sure everything was intact. Rick was always doing his job, and took it one step further to go beyond the call of duty. He worked tirelessly to help me, and was a true friend throughout it all. The patience, devotion, and energy he gave during those six weeks was remarkable.

I could tell by Rick's demeanor that the X-rays revealed what I expected, that everything looked good. By that point, I'd taken numerous X-rays of my ankle because of the surgery, and I had developed a pretty good feel for reading them. I could see that the screws were straight, but the plate had become slightly bent from all the pressure. I was assured that the bent plate was not a problem, and that all was well.

Actually, things were better than that. The X-rays made it official: I took the risk of suffering a career-ending injury to play in the Super Bowl and came through unharmed. Although I had confidence that God was looking out for me and protecting my leg, I admit I felt a measure of relief that the danger was over. I had made it through the woods.

Before leaving, I talked to a bunch of the guys in the locker room and thanked them for believing in me. I then braced myself for the media barrage and entered their den.

I told them, "A lot of people in the world didn't believe I could play, but my faith alone—the power of prayer and the power of faith carried me all the way."

Of course, I was also motivated by the chance to play in and win a Super Bowl. I wanted a ring, a Super Bowl Championship ring. I wanted to prove the doubters and haters wrong. I wanted to show everyone who believed in me that they were right. All of that was important to me as I got started with my rehabilitation.

Along the way, I became motivated by something else. I was surprised by how much attention my injury received. The experts said I couldn't do it. The doctors said I couldn't come back in six weeks from a surgery that requires ten weeks' recuperation. I was told by my surgeon that even if the ankle and fibula felt good, they were still fragile and could snap. The point is that I set out to do something that supposedly couldn't be done.

My purpose in rehabbing my leg wasn't to motivate other people; my focus was 100 percent on getting healthy enough to play. But once that happened, I saw that I had set an example for others to follow. I admit it felt good to show people that by having faith in God and themselves, they too could do what supposedly can't be done. I liked the idea of inspiring other people to help themselves. I wanted people in wheelchairs to believe that, through faith in God and themselves, one day they could heal, too. I wanted kids and adults with life-threatening illnesses to have faith and be positive. I wanted to make a difference in people's lives. I wanted to do good.

I am a religious person and I wanted to spread the word of God to anyone who could hear it. Some people said I was greedy for doing this. If that's being greedy, then I challenge those people to show me how my believing in God to find the strength for a tremendous accomplishment is anything but right.

The only thing greedy about my thoughts was that I wished my grandma, Alice Black, who suffers from Alzheimer's, could make a remarkable recovery, too. She hasn't. I guess no matter how much heart a person has, sometimes we have to play the hand that God has dealt.

With the spirit of Alice Black in me, I played my hand the best I could and felt justified after the game. I wasn't happy or in a great mood, since we'd lost the game, but I felt justified because I'd set things right in my world. To celebrate, I went to a Waffle House with my girlfriend Felisha, my friend Coop, and my friend and bodyguard Pablo. I wasn't in the mood for a celebration; I was physically exhausted and we'd lost a close game that we had plenty of chances to win. We lost because we couldn't capitalize on our opportunities and because the Patriots capitalized on theirs. Although I moved on, it was tough to think about how close we'd come to winning it all.

Over the next couple of days, I checked out ESPN.com and watched a lot of TV. I saw the headlines. The media gave me plenty of credit and then took their shots at me. They said I was spectacular in my effort to play and that I delivered an amazing performance. The articles and commentary were complimentary toward me, at first. Then they had to qualify everything and excuse themselves for being so positive toward me by mentioning something negative about me as well. Just about every compliment was accompanied by a backhanded insult. They called me controversial and brought up some previous incidents that had nothing to do with my Super Bowl performance.

At the end of one article that said how great I played there was actually an internet vote on whether I helped or hurt the team. I realized right then and there that I will never get a fair shake.

Regardless of what the media had to say, the coaches and players in that game spoke the truth. I got a lot of praise from the players; I appreciated what my teammates and opponents said on the record.

Patriot linebacker Mike Vrabel said, "For him to come back and play the way he played, I've got a lot of respect for him."

Coach Reid said, "TO did a heck of a job. I was proud of the effort and they battled, but we came up just short—too many turnovers—and against such a tough football team you can't do that."

Coach Reid hit the nail on the head. It's just too hard to beat a Super Bowl Champion team like the New England Patriots with all the turnovers.

Even Donovan could not help but be complimentary toward me, saying, "It's remarkable how he was able to come back and played so well for us."

To be fair, I believe that you win as a team and you lose as a team. The Super Bowl is the final game of a long season, a time when a player shows what he's made of, when everyone should be at the top of his game. Although many guys had strong individual performances, as a team, we came up short—end of story.

As politically incorrect as it is to say anything bad about Donovan, the media were somewhat critical of him. An Associated Press article I read on February 8 said the following:

McNabb was shaky at times in Sunday's game. He passed for 357 yards and three touchdowns, but he also threw three interceptions.

The quarterback misfired on several passes early, held the ball too long at other times, and made several poor decisions. One of the best scramblers in the NFL, McNabb had zero yards rushing on just one carry and was sacked four times.

He struggled in particular in the fourth quarter, getting picked off twice and looking slow in getting the team moving late.

Looking back at his performance, no matter what has been reported correctly or incorrectly, we all came up short on that team. A W is a W and an L is an L.

I don't care whether Donovan was tired or not, I cared about him trying his best and that's what he did. I tried my best and gave it everything I had, and yet despite having what was universally proclaimed a great game, I got a slap on the wrist for no reason other than being TO.

8

The Off-Season

A **PLAYER'S** true time off from football begins when the season ends, in January or February, depending on how far his team went in the playoffs. In my case, the season didn't really end until mid-February because I was invited and went to the Pro Bowl in Hawaii the week after the Super Bowl.

Then, in late March, we're required to report for off-season workouts. Most players have a clause in their contract that says they must participate in 90 percent of the workouts from March through June. There's usually a bonus provision built in if you meet the 90 percent threshold, though in some contracts the team can actually take money out of a player's salary if he doesn't hit that 90 percent requirement.

With the new Collective Bargaining Agreement, the NFLPA, among numerous other things, managed to get the NFL owners to agree that all new contracts executed by the start of the 2006 season cannot have any language that takes money out of a player's pocket for failing to meet a workout requirement. Now, owners can entice players to work out in the offseason by paying them a bonus rather than threatening to take money away. Although the NFLPA protected the players' wallets, the coaches still require a strong commitment. Most contracts require a four-out-of-five-day-per-week effort, every week from mid March through June. Each team's schedule in the offseason is different, some more difficult than others. Nevertheless, the offseason time for a player to kick back, enjoy himself, go back to school, or just spend time with his family is very short—as little as a month or two.

NFL coaches want all their players participating in their off-season program. The coaches want to know that the players are exercising properly and staying in shape, not just hanging out in their hometowns gaining too much weight or getting into trouble. It's good for the guys to be working out together from a team-bonding standpoint. If a young player wants to learn and improve, there's no better way to spend an off-season than to practice with the veterans who know what they are doing. From a coach's viewpoint, the off-season program gets everyone doing exactly what he wants them to do. Coaches don't like it when players do their own thing.

Some veterans—and I'm one of them—want to train harder and in a different manner than the coaches want. I'm in the shape that I'm in because I spend my off-seasons training in a more rigorous, demanding, custom-tailored exercise program than the group workout set up by the team trainers. Don't get me wrong, the teams set up excellent training programs; it's just that I'm used to a very specific regimen uniquely designed for my physique.

I can't blame the coaches for wanting to keep their players somewhere reasonably controlled. It's a big mistake for a young player, or an undisciplined one, to spend the off-season away from the team. It's easy for a player to get into trouble back in his hometown. There are always a lot of guys back home who are jealous of your success. The nobody back home wants to be somebody, and he sees picking a fight with the NFL big shot as a way to achieve that.

Sometimes the NFL player is really at a disadvantage, because the player can be at a hometown bar with his girlfriend or his wife, having a nice time, when some jerk comes along and insults the player—or even worse, the player's woman. I am not a violent person, but where I come from, when another man says or does something disrespectful to your girlfriend or wife, he has a butt-kicking coming to him. Then, when the player goes ahead and defends his honor or his family and friends, he can wind up arrested, jailed, sued, fined by the NFL, and possibly suspended. It could cost him hundreds of thousands (if not millions) of dollars between the civil lawsuit and fines from the NFL. That's why I usually have a bodyguard accompanying me wherever I go in public. My friend Pablo, who has a professional license now to do so, works as a bodyguard, as does my good friend Richard Halford (an Atlanta police officer)—not to protect me from getting beat up but to protect me from the trouble that would come from my beating up someone else.

I know that if I ever got into a fight with a fan who said or did some terrible things, the media would automatically blame me and say that the NFL's bad boy is at it again. If I get so much crap for doing things that are completely legal, imagine how much heat I'd catch if I were ever arrested for breaking the law.

Speaking of catching heat, I certainly caught some at the Pro Bowl in Hawaii. Not that kind of heat, but the kind on Peyton Manning's passes. I was still sore from the Super Bowl, but I wanted to spend a week in Honolulu with my family. I promised the Eagles and myself that no matter how tempted I got, I would not play in the game. I got pretty tempted, too.

I can't be around the action and not get into it. I couldn't help myself. So at the pregame exercises, I ran into Peyton Manning and couldn't resist catching a few passes from him. Catching passes from one of the best quarterbacks in today's game was definitely fun, and it's something I wouldn't have been able to do if I were playing in the game, since we're in different conferences. I ran full speed and went all out. Peyton hit me perfectly every time. I wanted to get a little taste of what Indianapolis Colts wide receiver Marvin Harrison had.

After running those routes, I kept my word to Rick Burkholder and shut it down. There was no way I could justify risking my career over a Pro Bowl game. Sure I was tempted to play, but it ended there at the pregame drills.

After catching some passes from Peyton in Hawaii, I returned to my off-season home in Atlanta to get some rest and relaxation. I still had the screws and plate in my ankle. It was time to sit on a couch and let it heal. I'm not much of a couch potato; I like to stay active. So that plan didn't exactly work out.

After having lived like a prisoner in an oxygen chamber for six weeks, I had to get out a little. I went to the NBA All-Star weekend and the ESPY Awards show. While at the ESPY show, I had the chance to talk with New England Patriots head coach Bill Belichick. He admitted to me that leading up to the Super Bowl he had asked his trainers if I would be able to play in the game. Belichick's trainers told him that there was no way. He said he was impressed with my ability to come back and how well I played in the game. That compliment, coming from one of the best coaches in the game today, meant a lot to me.

Between those events, I got a little break from the grind of the NFL schedule. However, on March 2, I had the second part of my surgery to remove the screws and plate from my ankle. They'd been inserted to strengthen and stabilize my ankle so it would heal properly, and they provided the support I needed to play in the Super Bowl. After the game, it was no longer necessary to keep them in there. In fact, I felt it was necessary to remove them because they restricted the motion in my ankle. Nevertheless, when the time came to part ways with them, I felt sentimental about the whole thing. Right before the surgery, I asked Dr. Myerson not to throw them away because I wanted to hang on to them as a souvenir. They were critical to my successful effort in the Super Bowl; I thought it would be a cool reminder to keep around the house.

As I was recovering from the surgery, I was a bit groggy. I remember someone coming into my hospital room to show me the two screws and the plate in a container. I asked the person to place them with the rest of my belongings. I was happy to have them.

When I got home, I laid out on my couch. The only time someone is going to catch me lying around is right after surgery. I'm a very active person with constant energy, and I like to keep moving.

Lying around the house, the day after surgery, I got introspective. I thought about my grandma's fight with Alzheimer's. I thought about my family as a whole. I started to think about my past.

It's strange what comes to mind sometimes when you're doing nothing. I remembered back to a girl I had liked when I was in the sixth grade. I had a crush on her and liked her all year long. One day in school, I finally mustered up enough courage to pass her a note during class. The note read: "Do you love me?" It had "Yes" and "No" boxes for her to check. She checked the "Yes" box, and I was very excited. I was shy toward girls and it took a long time for me to make my move. She was the first girl I ever liked. It was the greatest news in the entire world when I got her note back.

Unfortunately, another boy in class liked her, too. She liked him all along. Me being the tall, not-so-good-looking, too-skinny kid that I was, she dumped me that same day. That was heartbreak city for me.

Eventually I got over it. In high school, I fell for a girl named LaTonia who was a year older than me. I had liked her for a long time before I started dating her. I waited too long; she had signed up to join the military and was leaving pretty soon after we started spending time together. I wanted her to be my first real girlfriend. Right before she left, we took a picture together and she wrote on it that I should wait for her. She promised me that when she got back we would be together.

I waited for her but she never came back to me. LaTonia's life was tragically cut short overseas in a military accident. I felt real pain over her passing for a long time. Still do.

The emotional type of pain made me prefer the physical type. I started thinking of the pain I went through from the initial surgery, and I got the itch to check out my screws and plate. I managed to hobble around and go upstairs into my bedroom. I checked the bag that had my belongings from the hospital. I found the container with the screws and plate inside.

I took the metal items out, held them in my hand, and took a good look. Something wasn't right. Upon further review, they didn't seem to be my screws. During the process of getting numerous X-rays between the two surgeries, I learned how to read the film to a decent extent. Along the way, it was pointed out to me how the plate had become slightly bent. I saw that on the film. I remembered what they looked like and knew these screws and plate weren't mine.

The screws and plate that were given to me seemed brand-new. I thought someone was trying to pull a fast one on me. I called the Eagles' trainer Rick Burkholder, and he set up a phone conference with Dr. Myerson. I reminded Dr. Myerson that I'd told him I wanted the screws and the plate as a souvenir, and told him that I didn't think I had gotten the right ones.

Dr. Myerson said he didn't know what had happened, but that the screws and the plate happened to be on his desk. There had to be some kind of mixup, he presumed.

I received the screws the next day.

I started to wonder, does everybody have to try to screw me (no pun intended)?

It was also around this time that I started noticing that more and more people were coming to me to complain about my agent, David Joseph.

During the season, people would call me and say that they wanted to do this marketing opportunity or that, but nothing ever happened. I would talk to David about it, and he said the deals fell through.

I had several different business endeavors going on while I was playing with the Eagles. David had certain responsibilities, and I got a lot of complaints about his handling of those responsibilities. I made various assumptions that my affairs were well in order; they weren't. I started to get a bad feeling about things. David was in charge of everything. He handled my NFL contract, my public relations, my marketing and endorsements, my investments, my bills, my taxes, and certain legal work. He oversaw all of these areas and was responsible for them.

What if he mismanaged them? I started to become very concerned and looked into everything.

To make a change, I brought Kim Etheredge into the picture as my publicist. I look at Kim as the female version of me—a good person, strong-willed, determined, and the best at what she does. Kim is a very professional, successful publicist whom I had known casually as a friend of a friend. I would run into her from time to time at various events. She commanded my respect right away because she means business and gets things done. She struck me as honest and hardworking. I told her a little bit about what was going on and asked her to check things out.

Working with NFL players, in my opinion, is a man's business. I don't think that's a sexist opinion; it's just that my teammates, coaches, and executives are men. There is a lot of male chauvinism going on. What I like about Kim is that she's tougher than any of them. She knows that people love to judge a book by its cover, so when this five-foot-four-inch woman comes in the door, they don't take her seriously. But believe me—her bark is as big as her bite! I knew she would be the right man for the job.

It didn't take long for her to realize that things were messed up.

David was more than my agent, he was my close friend. He was like family to me. When I saw the true state of my finances, I realized that I did not have the financial security I thought I had. I was devastated.

I showed David unquestioned loyalty during the botched free agency situation. If he had just mailed in that letter when I signed it, I wouldn't have been in that mess. I would have had a different contract than the one he urged me to sign. I would have had a different contract than the one the NFLPA urged me not to sign.

If he had just sent in the letter right away, I would have been a free agent at the start of free agency and been able to negotiate a fair market value contract.

If he had taken the same position as the NFLPA and advised me to become a free agent and not take the deal, once more I would have had a contract set by the market, not by David and the Eagles.

If I had just listened to my instincts, instead of my conscience, I would have turned down the Eagles' offer and gone into free agency.

I realized that the bad situation I was in was completely my fault, not David's. The ultimate responsibility was mine, so I had to act with a sense of responsibility for my future and that of my family.

I saw that David did what he could as a small "mom and pop" type of operation, but I needed the best in the business in all the different fields.

At first I thought that I had outgrown him. Then it became clear in black and white that he was not the friend I thought he was.

I blew it. I trusted a friend with business. I should have separated friendship from business. I'm loyal to my friends and I want them to be successful. I was loyal to a fault and paid a big price for it.

I wanted David to be like me—to go from the small time to the big time. I assumed that because I could do it, he could, too.

It turned out my affairs were botched and my friend had disappointed me—immensely.

I was as close to David as I was to any man on the planet. He was part friend, part brother, and part father.

I knew what I had to do—go bowling.

I had a first-class trip all set up for me to go to Miami and participate in an ESPN celebrity bowling event.

It turns out that Willis McGahee was at that event. Willis is a running back for the Buffalo Bills. Like me, he overcame an injury to be successful. Although we had that in common, Willis's situation was far different from mine.

Willis was The Man as a junior playing running back for the University of Miami. Toward the end of the fourth quarter in the last game of the year, Willis was on his way to entering the 2003 NFL draft and was likely going to be the second or third overall pick. He was about five minutes away from getting a $14-million bonus.

Unfortunately, Willis caught a short pass and as he tried to run with the ball, a defender hit Willis in the knee. Willis's knee buckled and was actually bent backward in one of the ugliest injuries I have ever seen.

I felt bad for him at the time and forgot about it for a while.

Then I heard that Willis was entering the draft and that his agent predicted he was going to be a first-round pick. When the draft came around, Willis was indeed a first-round pick.

It happened that Willis's agent, Drew Rosenhaus, was there at the bowling event. I had a couple of friends with me at the time. I didn't know much about Drew but they sure did.

One of my friends there had once considered becoming an agent. He knew everything about Drew and had much respect for him. He was really excited that Drew was there. My friends and I had just been talking about how bad my situation was. I knew I had to make a move away from David but didn't know where to go. The fact that Drew was there, and that my friends were so interested in him, made me think that fate was intervening.

Drew was there with his brother and partner Jason and their marketing director Robert Bailey. I thought it through and asked my friend to approach Drew and ask him to come over and talk with me about my situation.

I was very serious and all business toward Drew, Jason, and Robert. We talked briefly. After I initiated the discussions about Drew becoming my agent, Drew explained that he couldn't do anything for me until after I severed ties with David. I kept the conversation very brief and told Drew that I would get back to him.

I did not really know a lot about Drew, but I knew he and his crew were important. As interested as I was in Drew, nothing was going to happen until I spoke with David. The more I talked with David, the less I recognized him. It seemed very ironic to me that in the nine years I had known David, I never once had gone to his office. I had made the mistake of blindly trusting someone else to handle my business without seeing for myself what was really going on.

As we talked, I thought about all the history David and I had together, all the ups and downs over the years. What it came down to was my friend for over nine years betrayed my friendship. I was crushed. I still am.

9
A New Sheriff
in Town—Me!

ETTING go of David was a major change in my life. I realized that it was time to take charge of my own affairs. Rather than have a small-time guy managing big-time business, I decided to go out and hire the best in the business in each of the specialized fields.

I hired Kim Etheredge full-time to be my publicist and help me manage my daily affairs. I hired Drew and Jason Rosenhaus of Rosenhaus Sports Representation to be my agents. I hired Robert Bailey of KCB Marketing to be my marketing and endorsement representative. Robert was a cornerback for eleven years in the NFL before working with Rosenhaus Sports as the director of marketing. I hired Jeff Rubin of Pro Sports Financial to be my financial advisor. Jeff worked with several of my teammates who highly recommended his services. I hired Allan Lerner of Lerner & Pearce, P.A., to be my attorney. I now had five top firms, each specializing in its particular focus, to handle what one small office had been doing.

When I told Drew, Jason, and Robert that I had not made any significant monies from endorsements with the 49ers or in my first year with the Eagles, they were in shock. The only significant marketing dollars I saw were what the NFL Players

Association had independently secured for me. Robert Bailey changed that for the better.

My financial situation was not what I thought was, much to my detriment. I was disappointed when Jeff broke down for me the true nature of my investment portfolio.

Allan went to work to tie up all the loose ends and help ensure a smooth transition away from the old system.

I now had an effective, powerful machine working for me. I realized that although they were all among the best in the country, I was the boss. Although I respected their advice, the final decision was to be mine, not theirs. They worked for me and not vice versa. Nothing was to be done without fully informing me first. One of the big mistakes I had made in the past was to blindly trust someone else to handle my business. I was not going to make that mistake again. I knew from then on, I needed to be on top of everything myself.

Other than getting my finances in order, the first priority of business was to address my situation with the Eagles, and here's where things stood . . .

I woke up one morning in April and took a hard look at my contract. I knew that I was as good as any receiver in the league and that I should be paid as such. If I'm one of the best performers in the league, I should be paid just as much as my peers. I wanted to know who the highest-paid receivers were and where I fit in the standings. The other receiver some experts said was comparable to me was Randy Moss, so I expected to have a contract comparable to his.

My contract was a seven-year deal worth approximately $49 million. That seemed like a lot of money to me.

"How much was Randy's deal?" I asked.

Randy has an eight-year contract worth $67 million that he signed in 2001 after three years in the league. Over seven years, he would earn $55 million. So Randy would earn $6 million more than me over seven years. Although I believed

I deserved to be the highest-paid wide receiver in the NFL, $49 million seemed like a good enough deal to me.

But there's a second factor to consider here. I'd be thirty-two years old by the end of the 2005 season. How much of that $49 million was I guaranteed to get? It turns out, when I first signed the contract I was guaranteed only $2.3 million. Even though I had been paid an additional nonguaranteed $6.8 million that first season, it still looked low to me compared to Randy Moss's guarantee of $18 million. That difference seemed ridiculous.

The first year's salary and total bonus amounted to $9.16 million versus Randy's $10.56 million. Okay, that's pretty close—not worth complaining about. The second year's salary and bonus totaled $3.25 million in my contract. Randy's second-year salary and bonus was $8.62 million. So, the first two years of Randy's contract called for him to be paid a total of $19.18 million. The first two years of my contract totaled $12.41 million. That just didn't sit right with me.

I then looked at how many other receivers had bonuses and salaries in their contracts during the first two years that totaled more than $12.41 million. I wasn't even among the top ten receivers in pay the first two years of my contract. That downright bothered me, especially since the contract was for seven years without the option to void out and become a free agent. No wonder the NFLPA encouraged me to turn the Eagles' offer down.

I know that some players' monies are deferred a year or two, but that doesn't affect the bottom line. Ten receivers would make more money from their contracts than I would if we were all released after the second year of our deals. I can understand one or two players making more, but not ten. That was flat-out wrong.

Where was all the money in my $49-million contract? In the back end of the deal.

In the third year of the deal, I was supposed to make $8.3 million. That would bring my three-year total to $20.68 million. Randy's three-year total was $24.27 million.

The big problem I had was that I was thirty-one years old as I headed into the second year of my contract. Randy was twenty-five after his second year. It's realistic to think that Randy will earn the full value from start to finish. He had already earned over $37 million over the first five years of his contract and was set to earn another $8.25 million in 2006. Whereas, at thirty-one, I was only in my second year of the deal and was scheduled to earn $3.25 million in 2005. I knew I wasn't likely to see my contract from start to finish. It was seven years on paper only. My seven-year, $49-million contract was more like a two-year deal worth $12.41 million that wouldn't put me among the top ten receivers in the league over the first two years of the contract.

My deal was specifically structured by the Eagles so they could pay me at a bargain price compared to what the premier receivers in the league were making. The Eagles' president, Joe Banner, was very clever. There were two big bonus amounts, payable in the first year and the third year. (The third year had $7.5 million in nonguaranteed bonus monies.) That was not by accident, it was by design. The idea behind it was that the Eagles wouldn't have to pay me the second big bonus unless they wanted to. If I got hurt or if things just didn't work out, they could cut me after my second year and they would have paid me less than what the ten highest-paid receivers would make over the first two years of their contracts.

The team had complete power to cut me and not pay me before the big money kicked in the third year. My big seven-year contract was more like a two-year audition, with unenforceable promises beyond that.

Here I was, underpaid and not getting any younger. I had

just survived a potentially career-ending injury, and a bad hit on my rehabilitated ankle or fibula could still cut short my career. If I got hurt, they could just release me.

I had just helped take this team to the Super Bowl and was perhaps the best player on the team. They had failed to get to the Super Bowl three years in a row, but with me, they got there and could have won that game. I risked my career and my contract to play in that game and try to help this team win the Super Bowl.

The Eagles benefited tremendously from my contributions. I figured they could return the favor.

The bottom line is I realized that, in all likelihood, I was looking at playing for a two-year deal at the age of thirty-one where I was going to be released, and never see the big money on the remaining five years of the $49-million deal. Even if they kept me for a third year, and then cut me at age thirty-three, what kind of leverage would I have to get a blockbuster deal then? Certainly not as good as I would at age thirty-one.

I said to myself that I was healthy right now, but what if I wasn't healthy and got released after the second or third year of my contract? How much leverage would I have coming off a serious injury?

Don't get me wrong; I believe I can play at a dominant level for at least another five years because of the extremely strict workout regimen I keep. With the way I take care of my body and how I condition it, I expect to be a force in this league for many years to come. But I don't have any guarantees, do I? Things happen on the field that none of us can control.

If I were ever to have the leverage to get a fair contract, I figured it would be after I risked my career and long-term quality of life to help the Eagles win the Super Bowl. I felt the team should do the right thing and reward me for the great contributions I made and would continue to make.

I knew I had signed the seven-year contract just one year before, but I outperformed the contract. In the NFL, when a player underperforms his contract, that player gets released and the team doesn't have to pay him a dime because contracts in the NFL are not guaranteed. In 2003, former Eagle defensive end Hugh Douglas signed a five-year $27-million contract with the Jacksonville Jaguars. The Jaguars paid Hugh a $6-million signing bonus that year. In 2004, Hugh's knee condition degenerated, and he was released just one year after signing the contract. Hugh never saw the rest of that $21 million. A team releases a player the moment he underperforms. So the way I saw it, what's good for the goose is good for the gander. The same team that forces a player to take a pay cut for underperforming should also give a player a raise for overperforming. I outperformed what my contract was paying me, and I felt the Eagles should reward me with a new contract.

I wanted to send a hungry, aggressive agent into the Eagles' nest. I wanted someone who would fight for me.

Enter Drew Rosenhaus.

Drew went to work immediately. The plan was to meet with the Eagles to state our position, and at the right time, we'd present them with an offer that would pay me fairly. The Eagles sold a tremendous number of 81 jerseys and made a lot of money off me. I felt I was one of the biggest stars, if not the biggest, in the league at that time. I transcended being a wide receiver and I wanted to be paid for what I brought to the table. I believed I was the ultimate player and wanted to go for the ultimate contract.

Our strategy was not to make threats or turn this into an ugly fight. We wanted to keep things as civil as possible. We hoped that at the midnight hour, we could strike a compromise that both sides would be happy with. We hoped the Eagles would consider my point of view and value my performance enough to do something special for me.

If that didn't work out, we would quietly stick to our guns, avoid the media, and play the situation out. If the Eagles were unwilling to redo my deal, then all options were on the table, including holding out of training camp once the preseason started. Holding out was an option, but it wasn't a concrete plan because that's a decision best made looking at all the facts at that time when training camp starts. We were not going to cross that bridge until we got there.

The moment word got out that I'd fired David and brought in Drew, the media went crazy. Drew had the reputation of being a tough negotiator but also a dealmaker. He prided himself on being a closer. I knew this would be a rough assignment, and I needed someone with the guts to do it. I was confident Drew had what it took to get the job done.

The media found out that Drew was flying from Miami to Philadelphia to meet with the Eagles' president, Joe Banner. It didn't take a genius to figure out that I wanted a new contract.

On April 6, the *Philadelphia Daily News* reported:

Eagles president Joe Banner will meet today with Drew Rosenhaus, new agent for wide receiver Terrell Owens. There is an unmistakable hint of trouble brewing between the Eagles and the superstar. Banner said he isn't sure what to think about Owens' sudden ditching of agent David Joseph in favor of Rosenhaus. "I'm not going to get into the specifics at this time," said Rosenhaus. "Whenever I begin representing a player, I always like to sit down with a team and discuss my client's contractual situation." Asked what Owens didn't like about the deal, which is said to pay him about $13 million over the first 2 years and $8 million in the third year, Rosenhaus said, "That's really between me and the team."

Drew wasn't going to reveal the details of the negotiation to the media. The press refused to be ignored, and without hard facts, they speculated and blew up the meeting into a huge story.

So when Drew went into Joe Banner's office, the Eagles were not caught by surprise. Drew explained our position, that I got stuck in a bad deal because a letter was not mailed on time, that I delivered a great performance, that I risked my career to play in the Super Bowl, and that I was underpaid.

Joe, in very clear, unmistakable terms, told Drew that they were not interested in renegotiating my contract. Joe explained that they could not renegotiate a seven-year contract after just one year. Joe didn't want to set a precedent that would encourage other agents to walk into his office and rip up their contracts because their clients had a good year. He told Drew that giving me a new contract would lead to chaos for the Eagles.

Drew countered that I was perhaps the best player in the league and that my contract grew out of extremely rare circumstances. Drew explained that this was a special case that could be explained to the other players as an exception to the rule.

Joe responded by reiterating management's position that there was not going to be a new deal, and that I had the option of either playing under my existing contract or not playing at all.

The Eagles' front office is definitely among the most respected in the league for being hardnosed. They are known for being very firm, and not budging. They were certainly the toughest team to go up against. Their initial uncompromising response was not a surprise.

When Drew concluded the meeting and walked out of the Eagles' complex, he was mobbed by a horde of media. Drew, not known for his shyness in front of TV cameras, didn't say much, since we wanted to keep the negotiations out of the media.

Drew didn't talk and neither did I or the Eagles. So the media did it instead.

Tony Kornheiser, on his ESPN show *Pardon the Interruption,* said, "You don't hire Drew Rosenhaus to restructure . . . you hire Drew Rosenhaus to rip up and get more."

ESPN insider Sal Paolantonio has the monopoly on the Eagles. I don't know who on the Eagles he talks to, but he gets the inside scoop from the highest authority. When people want to know what's going on with the Eagles, they turn to Sal.

After Drew's meeting with Joe, we knew that Sal would give us the best reading on what the Eagles' front office was really thinking. He reported the following on April 12:

PHILADELPHIA—It has been five fun-filled days of sports talk in this town since Terrell Owens dumped his longtime agent and friend, David Joseph, and hired the intrepid Drew Rosenhaus, who showed up at the Eagles Novacare Complex last week as if he were Ashton Kutcher in the hit movie, "Guess Who.". . .

On Wednesday, Rosenhaus met with Eagles president Joe Banner. Owens' current contract, which runs through 2010 and which Owens signed last year, is worth about $6.9 million per year, about the third-highest average salary for a wide receiver (behind Marvin Harrison and Randy Moss). But, after making about $9 million last year, Owens is due about $3.5 million in 2005.

And in 2006, when Owens will be turning 33, he will be due bonuses totaling about $7.5 million. *No one believes the Eagles will fork over that money to a player that age* [emphasis added]. . . .

Just ask the agents for Jeremiah Trotter and Duce Staley, or Bobby Taylor or Troy Vincent or Ike Reese. All were extraordinarily productive and wildly popular, but once they reached 30, they had to get their money elsewhere (Trotter may be back in Philly, but Banner never gave in).

There it was, in black and white on paper. The foremost expert on what the Eagles were most likely going to do wrote: "And in 2006, when Owens will be turning 33, he will be due bonuses totaling about $7.5 million. No one believes the Eagles will fork over that money to a player that age."

Sal went on to write that although it was not likely, there was a remote possibility that the Eagles might give in and compromise because they needed me to be happy in order for the team to have a successful season. I hoped some kind of compromise was in the mix, but Joe made it extremely clear the Eagles were not going to compromise in any way, shape, or form whatsoever. They took a hard-line approach against me.

Now I had just played in a game that could have cost me my career. Although I had tremendous faith and confidence that I would come through, I couldn't ignore the threat. I did not want to just play out the 2005 season at the risk of getting injured and winding up with nothing.

I felt that I had to take a stand. And they felt they had to do the same. So the stage was set for a monster battle of wills. The Eagles had their reasons for doing what they did, and I had mine. The media predicted that it was very unlikely that the Eagles would redo my deal. I believed with all my heart that I deserved a new contract. In order for me to have the type of financial security I had mistakenly thought I already had, I needed a new contract. Being the ultracompetitive person that I am, I had a conviction that I was right to fight for a new deal. I wasn't going to back down just because they had said no. We hoped there'd be room for a compromise as the process moved forward, but I had to be ready for a tough fight if we were to make that happen. It was time to buckle up and brace for impact, because the Eagles and I were on a collision course.

10
The Principle

AFTER Drew's meeting with the Eagles, there were a lot of different reports and opinions out there. I came across a lot of fans accusing me of being selfish for wanting a new contract.

I know that the average fan who works hard making thirty thousand to fifty thousand dollars a year at a nine-to-five job to support his or her family is never going to feel sorry for someone "stuck" in a seven-year $49-million contract. They're not going to sympathize with my point that I'm only making $3.25 million in 2005. I understand that to them—and to me—that's a tremendous amount of money, and I can see how my position could look ridiculous to them.

I'd ask them to give thought instead to what's right and wrong. It's all about what's fair. I won't argue with anyone who says I make a lot of money, and that teachers and fire-fighters and sanitation workers should make a lot more money than they do—but if I get less money than I'm worth, that money isn't going to go into the pocket of a teacher or firefighter, it's going to stay in the pocket of an extremely rich man who owns a pro football team. Team owners want fans to think that player salaries have a significant effect on ticket prices, but ask yourself: When was the last time a team reduced its prices when it was reducing its payroll? Ticket prices follow only one law, the law of supply and demand.

One of the first arguments that people make against me is that I signed a long-term contract one year ago and I should honor it. To dishonor that contract because I'll only make $3.25 million in 2005 is wrong, from their viewpoint. I admit that on the surface of things they're right.

Before jumping to any conclusions, I ask you to have an open mind and be objective in listening to my viewpoint. Forget about me, my controversial actions, and that I'm an NFL player for this one moment. I just want to ask this one question: Wouldn't any employee want a raise if circumstances had created a situation in which the employee was unfairly underpaid?

The honest answer is yes.

Whether that employee is scheduled to make $32,500 or $3.25 million is completely irrelevant to the question of what's right and wrong. The true debate is whether I was unfairly underpaid or not.

A person is unfairly underpaid when that person's peers make more than he or she does for the same work and performance.

Let me ask this follow-up question:

If one employee, Alice, works harder, more efficiently, and more productively to have a greater value to the company than another employee, John, who has the same job, is it right that Alice make less than John?

I don't think so. Would it be unfair if ten other employees, who have the same job as Alice and contribute less to the company than she does, end up being paid more than she is? I think it would be unfair.

Yes, there is a point to honoring a contract; but there is also a point to asking to renegotiate an unfair contract.

If Alice, who was making $32,500, went to her boss and

said that ten other people in her department, who did not contribute as much to the company as she did, were making more than she was, and then asked her boss for a raise, would the public sympathize with her or the boss?

Everybody except management would be in favor of her being rewarded.

How about if Alice's current contract was negotiated by an attorney who was incompetent, negligent, and screwed her over? Wouldn't the whole world agree that she deserves a new contract?

And how about if she had put forth the single greatest performance in the history of her position in that company?

And how about if that company had an amazingly successful year because of her performance?

And how about if the other employees all performed better because she helped make them better?

And what if she broke her leg and worked unbelievably hard to get back to work and delivered a heroic performance in the biggest meeting of the year?

And how about if Alice couldn't just quit and go work somewhere else because Alice's industry has an agreement that keeps her from finding another employer who'll pay her what she deserves, and all she can do is retire if she doesn't like it?

How would you feel if Alice was starting to get a little old for the job and only had several years left? Wouldn't you want her to get as much money as she was entitled to for as long as she could justifiably earn it?

No fair, open-minded, objective, honest reader can disagree with any of that.

So why am I different?

It's because I'm making millions of dollars instead of thousands. That's where it starts. The problem is that people care about the amount of money I make. That is all they see.

I know that I'm extremely blessed. I've worked my butt off to succeed in a tough and demanding sport, but I'm fortunate to have the God-given skills that game demands and to live in a time when players are well compensated for their efforts. The NFL generates an enormous amount of money, and the NFLPA has fought hard for the players to make an increasingly reasonable share of those dollars. We are the game; we have the unique abilities that make this a game that people love to watch.

My momma and my grandma weren't so lucky. They spent their lives working in a mill, putting up with nasty conditions and ugly remarks because there were few employers in town, and they knew that they were replaceable as workers but not as providers of food and shelter for their family. They had no choice but to accept things that were unfair. I have a choice; I can't be replaced so easily, or at all. So I'm in a position to do something they wished they could do, to stand up for what I believe is right.

Why do people care if I make millions of dollars? With some of the people out there, it's probably jealousy, but with others I think it's because even the lower amount of money I was scheduled to receive would be enough to make them happy.

Personally, I don't think Alice would be satisfied making $3.25 million if her peers were making more, especially if she was better than they were. I haven't heard of too many high-powered executives at IBM or any other big corporations who are happy doing more work for less pay than other executives. Isn't there the principle of equal pay for equal work? Doesn't that apply to athletes, too?

I have seen many famous actors and TV personalities take shots at NFL players for wanting to get paid big money. I find it extremely ironic that actors making ten to twenty million off one movie criticize football players making a fraction of what they make. I haven't noticed too many Hollywood actors breaking their fibulas and requiring screws drilled into their ankles while acting on the set.

Don't get me wrong, I have a lot of respect for actors and hope to do more of that myself down the road, but let's keep it honest.

People who were critical of me for wanting to renegotiate said I was all about the money. I think they got it wrong. They're the ones who are all about the money. To them, I was wrong because I was already making millions of dollars. That was the reason most of my critics were against me. They couldn't imagine being unhappy making so much money. They think that when the money's that good, there shouldn't be questions about fairness or right and wrong.

On the other hand, I didn't care that I was already making big money, I wanted what was right. If my contract was at the top of the market and paid me fairly, then I wouldn't be fighting for a new one. Of course I would have honored the contract. My problem was the principle that I was underpaid and I wanted what was fair.

I put the principle over the principal. So, the way I see it, anybody who tells me that I am about the money isn't smart enough to realize that they're actually the ones who are about money.

A lot of people who criticized me said I should "honor the contract." Those are interesting words. I'll say this plainly: I would have been thrilled to honor my commitment to play seven years for the Eagles at $49 million as advertised. But that's not how NFL contracts work. A lot of football fans don't realize that unlike NBA and Major League Baseball contracts, player contracts in the NFL are not guaranteed. The team can always drop you if they think you're overpaid, no matter how much time is left on your contract. They built their own right to dishonor their commitments right into the contract! Sal

Paolantonio, the Eagles guru, said they were unlikely to honor more than two years of the deal themselves. Sal said that I wasn't going to see the $7.5-million bonus I was scheduled to get in the third year of my contract; they were going to cut me after two years, getting my best years at a bargain price. They were going to chew me up and spit me out as they have all their other great players once they turned thirty. They were going to throw me out on the street whether I was injured or not. Maybe they might have kept me one more year, but then after getting released I would have had no leverage.

One thing every veteran learns the hard way is that there is no loyalty in this business. No one can say otherwise. Teams will cut the greatest person and player in the world the moment he becomes overpaid and obsolete. There's a reason that Joe Namath wound up his career with the Los Angeles Rams, Johnny Unitas with the San Diego Chargers, Joe Montana with the Kansas City Chiefs, Franco Harris and Jerry Rice with the Seattle Seahawks, and Ronnie Lott with the New York Jets. Pro football is a business, and that's just how businesses are run.

So in a league with no loyalty, Joe Fan says that I should have loyalty to the team and honor my contract. He thinks that I should honor my contract as a matter of principle. But what kind of principle operates in only one direction?

Critics argued that if I was so concerned about getting cut in 2006, why not play out 2005, have a great season, and then go out on the market when the Eagles released me?

I didn't want to play out 2005 for $3.25 million only to get cut afterward, because I couldn't win. First and foremost, if I played the 2005 season under my existing contract and got hurt, I would get cut and could wind up with nothing if I reinjured my fibula or ankle. That was not an appealing option. I did not want to take the risk, and I felt that, after everything I'd done for the Eagles, I shouldn't have to.

Second, if I did play out the 2005 season and had a tremendous year, I'd be fine with the Eagles' releasing me, because I believed I would get more as a free agent than the money I was scheduled to make under my Eagles contract. But guess what? They would still have the option to keep me and steal me at an undermarket contract price, and I couldn't go out and get what I was worth. So if they kept me in 2006, taking money out of my pocket, I would then have to play out that season and face the same situation all over again. And I could still get hurt in 2006 and wind up with nothing more. That seven-year contract had no clauses allowing me to get out of it down the road. The team had total control over my rights, as if I were property, not a human being. They had all the options.

For all these reasons, I had to try my hardest to get a new contract. For all these reasons, I thought the Eagles should compromise with me. For all these reasons, I was very angry that they refused.

Without a new contract or any show of good faith, I decided not to participate in the voluntary off-season program. Critics said I needed to be there to be in shape to start the season. One thing nobody can question is my commitment to being in shape and being ready to play football. Yet I was hearing people criticize my performance, my work ethic, and my commitment to winning. I didn't think that was fair. Out of frustration, I responded on April 12 in a conversation with ESPN reporter Len Pasquarelli:

> As always, there is a lot being written and [reported] without anyone talking to me. I mean, I can't do right and I can't do wrong. It's getting, in some ways, like it was for me in San Francisco. But the one thing that won't change is that I'm going to show up to play and to win. No one can ever [debate] that. . . .

No one can ever accuse me of not being in great shape. Andy knows that. My teammates know that, when I show up, I'm ready to go. The biggest concern should be winning a Super Bowl. That's what I show up to do. I've never been out of shape. I mean, this is my [livelihood]. . . .

[Regarding the Super Bowl,] I was trying to inspire myself. I wanted to prove to myself that I could do it. But why did I want to do it? To win a Super Bowl for the team, for the fans, for the city. I did everything they asked me to do. I played every snap they allowed me to play. I wasn't even running until, like, two weeks before the game. But I made sure I was in the best shape possible. I wasn't the guy who got tired in the Super Bowl.

The next day, the papers all said I took a shot at Donovan. I didn't mention Donovan's name, but they all assumed I meant Donovan. I talked to Len for a while and said a lot of things to him. That one last sentence was all anybody noticed. I didn't go into that conversation thinking that I was going to say something negative about Donovan. I admit that it looks that way. I admit that at the time, I was angry with Donovan, but when Len asked me if I was talking about Donovan, I would not say I meant Donovan.

Everybody knows I speak my mind and don't pull any punches. If I meant to take a shot at Donovan I would have said yes when Len asked if that was who I was referring to.

I did not say, "Donovan got tired at the Super Bowl," nor was it my intent to do so. To understand what I meant, you have to understand how I communicate. The best way to describe it is that I operate like a sponge. I soak up what's around me and when pressed, I let out what I took in. Other players said that Donovan got tired in the Super Bowl—on the record and off the record. He denied it publicly, and I didn't care if he was telling the truth or not. I wasn't trying to call Donovan a liar or embarrass him; I was just kind of regurgitating the talk going around, and my main point was being made in my own defense, because it was my conditioning that was being criticized. I was talking about me, and no one else. I was the one who should have been tired in the fourth quarter, since I didn't have the chance to start running and conditioning myself into game shape until about two weeks before the Super Bowl. Due to my hardcore conditioning and extreme work ethic, I didn't get tired. It was outrageous that my conditioning was being questioned. I was just reminding people that if anyone could have been expected to get tired, it was me.

I have been severely criticized for speaking my mind and not tempering my words. If I had meant to talk about Donovan, I would have made that clear. I wasn't trying to insult Donovan. It was a slip of the tongue, and if I could take it back I would, but I can't. Still, when Len asked me to say Donovan's name, I wouldn't.

When Hank Fraley said that Donovan got tired and Freddie Mitchell confirmed it on the record, no one made that big a deal out of it. So when I said something that seemed similar (without mentioning Donovan's name), I didn't think it was a big deal either.

It never occurred to me that the media would want to create a me-versus-Donovan situation. I never dreamed that what I said would turn into the monster story of the off-season. All I meant was that nobody should question my work ethic, and that I would be ready to play on Sundays. I didn't have some strategic plan to insult their golden boy as a way to magically inspire the Eagles to rip up my contract and give me a big raise. That would be a pretty stupid plan. Yes, there were problems between me and Donovan, but I didn't want to say something that would publicly offend and humiliate him. I made a poor choice of words.

If that was how people chose to take it, that was their problem. If anyone has a problem with it, just come to me and let's talk about it. If Donovan had called me to ask me about it, I would have told him I didn't mean to say anything that publicly embarrassed him.

I wish he had come to me, because we could have cleared the air between us, and that would have helped out everybody. But he didn't come to me and I didn't go to him. He never apologized to me for embarrassing me in the huddle in the Giants game. He never apologized to me for getting defensive and confrontational in the locker room. He never apologized for walking away from me in the locker room. He never apologized to me for not being supportive during my rehab process. He never apologized to me for making it seem to the media that I was not important to the team's chances of winning the Super Bowl. Before I made the "tired" remark to Pasquarelli, I could have used Donovan's support in trying to get a new contract; he didn't support me. He wasn't in my corner. For all of these reasons, I didn't see any reason to apologize to him.

What I didn't consider is that I said something publicly that caused embarrassment to my teammate. Even though I didn't mean to say something that would have that effect, it was wrong. For that, I should have apologized, but I couldn't bring myself to do it, and I refused to consider any point of view other than my own. That was a mistake, and if Donovan and I ever sit down with good intentions, I will apologize to him for that.

A bigger problem was that after I said something so politically incorrect, public opinion turned on me. Before I made that comment, there was some public support for my position; after the comment, there was almost none. Only Michael Irvin had the conviction and the guts to stand up for me. Everyone else just blew with the wind, and said whatever they thought their audience wanted to hear.

After I made that controversial commercial, one fan showed her approval when I caught a pass for a touchdown against the Packers in Philadelphia. *(AP Photo/Rusty Kennedy)*

I was still recovering from surgery but was ready to celebrate when the Eagles defeated the Falcons to win the NFC Championship on January 23, 2005. *(AP Photo/Rusty Kennedy)*

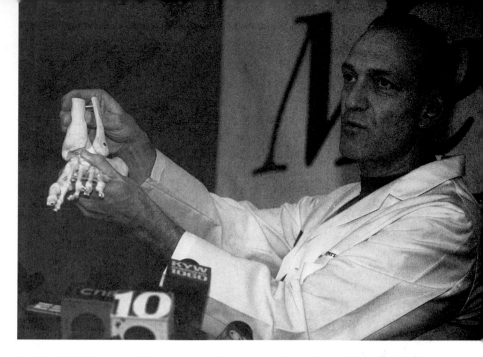

Dr. Mark S. Myerson, the surgeon who operated on me on December 22, 2004, to repair my torn ligaments. Most observers thought there was no chance I could play in the Super Bowl after this surgery.
(*AP Photo/Chris Gardner*)

On February 1, Media Day, there were plenty of reporters who wanted to hear me say that I would be ready to play in Super Bowl XXXIX.
(*AP Photo/Stephan Savoia*)

I worked incredibly hard to rehab in time to play in the Super Bowl game in Jacksonville. I did my best to avoid tacklers during the game, but they still found me. *(AP Photo/David J. Phillip)*

That's my agent, Drew Rosenhaus, surrounded by reporters on August 1, 2005, the day I reported to the Eagles training camp. I wasn't happy about my contractual situation, but I was always in shape and ready to play. *(AP Photo/Coke Whitworth)*

Ten days later I was dismissed from training camp, and I stayed in shape by shooting baskets at my home. Somehow the media found me again. *(AP Photo/Courier-Post, John Ziomek)*

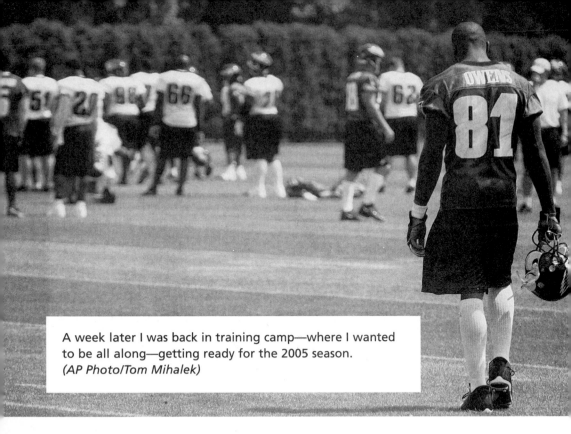

A week later I was back in training camp—where I wanted to be all along—getting ready for the 2005 season. *(AP Photo/Tom Mihalek)*

With Drew Rosenhaus alongside me, I read a statement to the media outside my home apologizing for my comments in an ESPN interview. *(AP Photo/Rusty Kennedy)*

I waved to reporters as I arrived for the arbitration hearing on November 18. I was feeling pretty good about my chances for reinstatement with the Eagles until I heard what the arbitrator had to say. *(AP Photo/Bradley C. Bower)*

NFL Players' Association head Gene Upshaw was also unhappy about the arbitrator's ruling in favor of the Eagles. *(AP Photo/Mark Stehle)*

Starting over: Owner Jerry Jones and I hold my new Dallas Cowboys jersey on March 18, 2006, as the Cowboys announced my three-year contract. *(AP Photo/Ron Heflin)*

Shortly thereafter, the Eagles had a mandatory minicamp, which I did not attend. As expected, the media made it into a huge story that I didn't go. I decided not to participate because I didn't want to risk getting injured, and I wanted to send the Eagles a message that I was serious.

As big a story as it was that I was not there, it became an even bigger story when Donovan responded to my comments and absence by saying the following:

> I don't play games in the media . . . I'm not going to sit here and try to have a war of words. I'm a man at what I do. If there's a problem with anyone, and they feel the need to lash out, they know how to get in touch with me and we can handle it like men . . .
>
> If you say I was winded, if you say the [offensive] line was winded, if you say the defense was winded, that's fine. . . . But to be tired and dropping to a knee, that didn't happen.

First, when I had a problem with him after the Giants game, I approached him like a man, and he did not do the same. Rather than address my issue, he disregarded me and walked off to do an interview. Second, I did not say that Donovan was tired and dropped to a knee. Third, after saying he wasn't going to play games in the media and have a war of words, Donovan went on to say the following:

> Just keep my name out of your mouth. Don't try to throw names or guys under the bus to better yourself. You never heard me say any names in any situation. You never heard me talk about any given players. I'm the guy to be professional and be a man about things.
>
> If a comment was made about me, it would take that person to call me. I don't have to reach out to anyone.

I must have missed the part where I mentioned Donovan's name when I said I wasn't the one who got tired. Rather than call me or approach me after I made my comments, as I did with him in the locker room, he chose to say some harsh words to reporters about me. Things went from bad to worse. The media ran with our comments, turning them into a big feud. Although I was conflicted and there was something bad between us, I was still confident that we could be successful on the field together. I did it with Jeff Garcia, and I could do it with Donovan.

After Donovan's comments, the Eagles' management reiterated on the record that I would either play this season under my existing contract or I would not play at all. They were not going to budge an inch.

With training camp fast approaching, the sporting world waited to see whether I would be there in July. The rumor mill had it that I was going to refuse to report for the start of training camp. Showing up without a new contract would be a very tough pill for me to swallow. I had a hard decision to make.

11
Training Camp

As training camp approached, I had to decide whether to report to camp. If I reported, the Eagles would have little reason to redo my contract. If I showed up and played, why would they pay me more than they had to? Option number two was not to report and to hold out. I was confident that, without me there, the coaching staff would realize they needed me to win a Championship—but the team could fine me thousands of dollars for every day I held out. Additionally, missing one day of camp could possibly put me in violation of my contract and potentially cause me to have to repay part of my signing bonus. It was one thing to miss a mandatory minicamp in the off-season—that could be smoothed over—but missing training camp was a different matter. This was serious, but so was I. I really went back and forth; one day I was prepared to hold out and another I was ready to report.

Through it all, I knew the smart move was to show up. The Eagles are a very strong-willed team, but I'm strong-willed, too. If I didn't show, they would fine me, and it would lead to a standoff that would end up with them taking money out of my pocket. I knew that they couldn't set the precedent of giving a new contract to a veteran player who was holding out. I knew that they wouldn't budge if I held out.

Donovan wasn't exactly in my corner on this one. He told the media:

> I feel that if he plays or not, we definitely have a chance of making it to the Super Bowl and winning it. . . . He has a contract. There is desire to have more money and there is the desire to lose money. That would at least give you the motivation to get back out there on that field. When you sign your name on the dotted line, that's your deal, and that's a decision you have to make.

I expected as much from Donovan. I guess he was pretty confident that the Eagles' offense could be successful without me. I knew otherwise and so did the Eagles' front office, but it was clear they weren't going to give in.

I thought a good compromise would be to trade me to another team. This way, they could get another good receiver to replace me, and I could get a new contract from another team. Plus the Eagles would be able to trade me to a team outside their division or conference, making the transaction more appealing to them since they wouldn't have to play against me or strengthen a division rival. This way, both sides would win.

I said as much to the media:

> When it all boils down to it, I'm doing what's best for my family. Not to stir anything up, but I don't really have to play for the Eagles, to be honest. I can go play with any other team and still be productive . . . I have no gripes, no ill feelings toward any of the players on that team. This is business. They know how business is conducted. I've told them what I'm doing is for my family . . . I feel like we can be adults about it. Trade me. Release me, and we can part ways like adults.

That made sense to me, but the Eagles were not interested in a trade. Joe Banner explained to Drew that if they traded me, that would set a precedent allowing any player who wanted out of his contract to demand a trade. That, too, was something the Eagles didn't want to do.

If they weren't going to give me a new contract, restructure my contract, guarantee the 2006 bonus, or trade me to one of several teams that would, there were no options for me other than to show up. I was not going to give them a reason to fine me. I made my decision and said the following to the media before the start of camp:

> I'll be there . . . I mean, the bottom line is that I still believe I deserve a new contract. I still believe I deserve more than what they've given me. But I'm not stupid. I'm not about to miss training camp, get fined every day and give them even more reasons to keep from paying me. I'll be there but I won't be happy, I can tell you that much. Take from that whatever you want.

Even after making that statement, I still wavered in my decision. I knew I would be there, but getting there was difficult. The media had a field day predicting whether I would show. When I did show up, they took their shots at me, saying that after all my threatening statements and posturing, I gave in to the Eagles by reporting. The thing was, I never said I wasn't coming to camp. I truthfully stated that I was undecided. I did the right thing, what I was supposed to do, and they criticized me for it. Had I not showed, they would have criticized me for that, too. No matter what I did or do, the media find an angle to criticize me. I understand that comes with the territory, but you can't expect me to like it. That's why I made the decision to completely shut things down and not talk to the media.

T.O.

As the midnight hour approached, I was in Tennessee to handle some personal problems. The plan was for me to drive from Tennessee to Atlanta and then fly from Atlanta to Philly. While making the two-hour drive, I was extremely emotional and thought about retiring. Don't get me wrong, I hadn't lost my love for the game, but the business side was becoming unbearable. Everything about reporting to camp was very unpleasant and unappealing to me. I knew I was going into a bad situation and that things were not going to get any easier. I didn't want to go and was tempted to turn around and spend more time with my family. I called my mom and Drew, telling them to be prepared for a press conference announcing my retirement. Just as I was struggling with the decision, I saw a sign for the University of Tennessee at Chattanooga—my alma mater.

I instinctively followed the sign to the school. Next thing I knew, I was walking around campus at two in the morning. I walked by the gym where I'd spent so much time exercising away my frustrations. I walked onto the football field where I had found my calling in life. I flashed back to plays I had made on that field. I visited my old dorm room where I had spent so many nights struggling to get through. This was where I grew into a man. Thinking back on everything I went through, what I overcame, and how much I'd accomplished since then, I felt a new strength within me.

A sense of pride overcame me and I was invigorated. No more contemplating retirement. I was ready to report. When I flew into Philly, and got with my mother, my friends Coop and Rich, Kim, and Drew all at my house, I was very emotional. I took great comfort in their support. They told me they loved me and respected my decision to face the music. When I left the house, I had a bittersweet moment when my mom hugged me as if I were going away for a long time into a dangerous place.

I decided to drive from the house to camp by myself so I could focus my thoughts and get my mind right for what lay ahead. As I drove into the facility, I felt anger toward management and the media. I felt that I was among the enemy. Dressed in a camouflage shirt and hat, wearing dark shades and headphones, I ignored the media as I made my way from my car into the lion's den.

The first order of business was for Drew and me to meet with Andy Reid and Joe Banner. Drew arranged the meeting, hoping that everything could be smoothed over and we could reach a mutual understanding. A good idea, but it didn't go down that way.

They made their point that they would not redo my deal or trade me. They made it clear that they weren't willing to compromise in any way. They had no intention of doing anything to make me feel better about the situation at all. In return, I told them that I was not happy with their position. I made it clear that I was going to honor my contract and work hard to win football games on Sundays, but that this wasn't going to be a good situation. The meeting did not accomplish what either side hoped it would.

I walked out feeling no better than when I walked in. I was not surprised, and despite what they had to say, I felt there was room for compromise. At that point, I would have been happy with any of several different alternatives available. They could agree to begin a dialogue to discuss a new contract as the season went along. They could trade me to one of several teams that were willing to pay me at a fair-market-value price. They could also agree to release me after the end of the season; that way I could have a great year for them and then have the chance to go on the open market and get a fair deal, perhaps even re-sign with them. Another option was they could have guaranteed part of my contract. I was willing to play out 2005 and risk losing it all to an injury if they would agree to any of those compromises. All of those options would have benefited both sides.

Unfortunately, the Eagles saw each and every one of those solutions as giving in to me and setting a bad precedent. The whole league was watching the Eagles, and I'm sure the club felt pressure to stand up to me. They were caught in a bad position.

At the time, I didn't care what their problems were. I felt it was worth it for them to work something out with me. They disagreed, and that drove me to the edge. As an extremely competitive person, I wasn't going to just lie down and take it. I was determined to do my job, but I was not going to take any disrespect from anybody!

I was angry and it showed. I felt that anybody who didn't support me was against me. The team trainer Rick Burkholder and my wide receiver coach David Culley were among the people who were understanding about my position. Most of the players were cool with the situation, and I didn't have any problems on the field or in the locker room. As for Donovan, he ignored me and I in turn ignored him. We did not speak.

I did what my contract required, but I wasn't going to sing and dance to make everybody happy about it. It was very difficult to be on bad terms with my coaching staff and quarterback. No player has ever had the guts to do that. But this was no longer about the money. This was about their having no respect for my position.

Although I refused to talk to the media, Drew made a statement that summed up the situation:

All the talk, all the rhetoric in the offseason is meaningless. . . . He's here. He's not happy with his contract, but he's a professional and he'll do his best to help the Eagles win a championship . . . Terrell is here to play football, he's very serious and businesslike. . . . Let me and the Eagles handle his concerns over his contract . . . We're not here to negotiate in bad faith or threaten to walk out. . . . This isn't about leverage.

Drew hit the nail on the head: I did what was required of me, but inside I couldn't help but feel that they should have done something for me. When they told me face to face that it is what it is and that's all, I could not just say okay and be fine with things.

The media, the Eagles' front office, the coaching staff, and the fans all eagerly waited to see how I would get along, or not get along, with my teammates at the first practice. My quarterback and I did not talk, we did not even say hello to each other. It wasn't necessary; the coach calls the plays to run in practice, and I ran them without having to interact with Donovan. When I stepped onto the field, there were some boos from the fans early on, but when I caught my first pass in practice, the crowd erupted with applause. Everything I did drew a reaction, and the fans were up and down with me. They were coming around. The only problem was that practicing and being part of the team did not make me feel any better.

I was unhappy for reasons having nothing to do with money. It was that they were getting the best of me. "They" were not so much the Eagles, but all of the media, the critics, and the jerks out there rooting against me. It bothered me that they opposed something that was extremely important to me. I didn't have to get what I wanted, but I deserved to get something. I got nothing. All the people out there hating on me were thrilled. Although they probably were hoping I would hold out, get fined, and eventually come in beaten, they were overjoyed at my frustration.

The only thing that motivated me was winning for my family. I wanted them to see me score touchdowns. I wanted my family to see me do celebration dances in the end zone. I wanted my family to feel good about my team winning football games and heading toward another Super Bowl run. I told myself that I should give my very best effort and everything would work out.

I was disappointed that Andy Reid and Joe Banner didn't think more of me. My anger toward Andy Reid the executive made me angry toward Andy Reid the coach. I couldn't separate one from the other. All the negativity from the outside began to fester on the inside.

To understand why I couldn't just accept "no" and like it, it's necessary to understand where I come from.

My grandmother Alice Black is the matriarch of my family. She was a single mother. All on her own, she raised my mother and her other children. She then helped my mother raise me and my younger siblings. She worked for many years at the Russell Mill, sewing clothes in the factory. It was the only steady job a single mother could get in Alex City, Alabama. She worked there for decades and barely made enough money to make ends meet. She was strict, but she was honest and principled.

Throughout the course of my grandma's life, she has suffered for many years from racism, from oppression, from poverty, from heartache; through it all she was a strong person. Her will could not be broken. She had to deal with bosses who were overbearing. She fought through terrible working conditions. She never quit, she kept her head high, and she always managed to support her family.

My grandma raised us all the best she could. She had to endure a lot in order to put food on the table. She couldn't fight back; all she could do was try to ignore it and rise above it. She suffered so we could better ourselves. She sacrificed everything for us, everything but her backbone. That woman's spirit could never be broken no matter how much injustice she had to deal with coming up in this world.

From Alice Black, I learned that adversity breaks the weak and makes the strong. By her, I was given an iron will that turned into steel when forged in the fires of anger.

There ain't nothing that the NFL can do to me that will ever break me. Alice Black never broke and neither will I. I fear no one, for I have faith in the Lord. I do what my conscience tells me and that is good enough for me. As long as Alice Black and my mother, Marilyn Owens, support me, I don't care what is written in the papers or said on TV.

I have no respect for the media anyway. Not just one, but many members of the media have tried to sneak down to Alabama and pry into my childhood. Through lies and manipulation, they've investigated the private lives of my family to get their story.

Reporters have popped up on the front doorstep of my mother's home, claiming to be doing a positive "Who Is Terrell Owens" piece. Once they gained her permission and got deep into the interview, they bombarded her with the kind of personal questions that were inappropriate. They'd ask about her relationship with my father and the circumstances of my conception. She'd get defensive, wanting to protect her baby, as any single mother who raised her firstborn on her own with only her mother's help would be.

It was challenging for us from the start. My mother was a young teen who got pregnant by a married, older gentleman who lived in the neighborhood. I got a call one day from my mother telling me that not only had a journalist printed this, but a popular African-American radio personality thought it should be the subject of the station's morning show. He made a joke out of it and insulted my mother and grandmother. He said I was "so messed up" because of the way I was conceived.

This hurt my mother's feelings. She felt pain because of the media. Not everyone she knew saw the article, but everyone listened to that disc jockey.

Who was he to talk about my family? What did they do to him? Was the gossip segment of his morning show so important that he had to stab in the heart a woman who had been wounded much of her life? She didn't deserve this and neither did my grandmother.

That wasn't the only time the media took a shot at my family. As for me, I can handle whatever they throw at me and it bounces off like nothing. But when it's my mother they are talking about it, and she gets upset, then I get upset. I take that as a personal assault, and I've had a growing dislike for the media ever since. They say and do whatever will make their bosses happy, no matter who gets hurt. They say and do whatever is good for ratings or subscriptions. Of course there are some prominent, responsible, high-character journalists, but they are more the exception than the rule.

To unnecessarily insult my family is just a cheap shot, and the people who did it should be ashamed of themselves. It's ridiculous for these same people to criticize single mothers and then characterize themselves as "serving the community."

All they're doing is hurting their viewers and listeners, because I'm not the only kid who had a single, teenage mother. Columnists, talk show hosts, and radio personalities should be trying to lift people, not bring them down. Oh, and by the way, the worst insult someone can offer a man is to talk about his mother. How would those clowns react if the shoe was on the other foot?

I know how I'd like to react, but that would only make things worse.

I realize that with the media it's all a business, but they don't have to get in my family's business. I don't have to play along and say what they want me to say and do what they want me to do. If I don't want to talk to them, I won't.

I am proud of my mother and have nothing to hide. I was

raised by two strong women. Although the circumstances may not have been ideal, my mother chose to bring me into this world and care for me alone. During my childhood I may have had some curiosity about my father, but as we say in the South, that was "grown folks' business" and it stayed that way.

I eventually met my father, under circumstances that were not ideal. When I was eleven years old, I had a crush on the girl who lived across the street. When my father found out about it, he told me I shouldn't think that way about that girl, and when I asked why not, he told me the girl was my half-sister, and that he was my father. That's how I finally learned who my father was.

It was hard for me to deal with, but my mother and grand-mother taught me to forgive those who sincerely asked for it. Just as I have with anybody who's apologized for not treating me right, I forgave my father.

Today my father and I speak regularly. We don't talk about what could have and should have been, only about the here and now. I can't go back into the past and fix it; I can only move forward with the present and accept it for what it's worth. Although my father's friendship and love were not there for me when I needed them as a child, they mean a lot to me today.

As I got into bed and stared up at the ceiling of my training camp dorm room, I thought back to the struggles we had when I was a child. My mother and grandmother worked their butts off day and night just so we could eat. After me came my sister Tasha, my sister Sharmaine, and my brother Victor. It was hard on all of us.

Momma and Grandma would sacrifice everything they had to make sure we got what we needed. I've said on several oc-casions that we didn't have much, but my momma could sew and she always made sure her children were clean and dressed properly. Even when Momma got her own place and took Sharmaine and Victor with her, I could still see the unhappiness on her face, wanting to do much more, wanting her children to live a better and different life than she did. She really wanted us to get out of Alex City.

Well, her wish came true. Thanks to them, we all have a better life. I honestly believe that God blessed me with great talent and success because of their deeds. It was their nurturing that gave me the heart and motivation I needed to achieve that potential. Don't get me wrong, all of my family is blessed, but I think I was destined to be my mother's shining star.

My momma once said to me, "I knew when you were a baby that you would be special. I knew that you would be different. Some sort of star."

Although I may not always say things the way others want to hear them, I have the voice these women didn't. My taking a stand against the toughest management in the NFL may have angered a lot of people, but it made my mother and grandmother proud. When I spoke up for myself, I was speaking for the Alice Blacks and Marilyn Owenses out there, who couldn't speak up for themselves. People called me selfish and much worse, but they don't know me. My friends and family know me, and they understand why I was so adamant about reaching a fair deal rather than just having the whip come down.

Today, my grandmother suffers from Alzheimer's. It's a dreadful disease. I've had to stand by and watch my loved one deteriorate right in front of me. I provide her with the best care money can buy, but there's still not much I can do. I've testified before the United States Congress about how destructive it is to see this debilitating disease slowly drain a person's life away from her.

My grandmother was always very strong. She set me in the

right direction and led the way for me. As I struggled over what to do in training camp, about just giving in and yielding, I thought of her. I wanted to talk to her, but I knew she couldn't lead me anymore.

I asked myself, what would my grandmother do? What would she want me to do? What can I do to make her proud? I had to rely on my memories of her and the values she instilled in me. Tears came to my eyes, and still do, as I thought of how she was when I was a kid and what this disease has done to her.

There is some measure of comfort in knowing that God has spared my grandmother from having to hear all the criticism I've drawn in the last year or so. The media have tried to embarrass me, shame me, and insult me. God is a good God, for he has shielded Alice Black from seeing her grandson, the young man she raised with an iron fist, bear the brunt of everything I've taken on.

I wanted so much to ask her one last time, "Grandma, what do I do?" I would do anything just to see her smile as she recognized my face. It's hard knowing that may never happen again. It's painful for me to slowly lose the real Alice Black, but the one thing I will never lose is the preparation she gave me to handle adversity in my life.

When I was a child, I watched her come home angry over the way she had been treated at her job. She told me never to let anyone walk all over me. She prepared me when she kept me away from my father, because she knew adults can disappoint children. She also prepared me to one day grow up and be an adult myself. She prepared me when she took that belt to my behind, to let me know that I have to be accountable for my actions. She prepared me by keeping me in the house all the time, to show me that not everyone I hung around with was a true friend. She prepared me by letting me know that when I have to stand alone, I won't be lonely because she and God will always be with me. I realize now that I am never alone. She may not be able to answer me if I ask her questions, but she no longer needs to. She's already answered them for me.

Her heart, her spirit, and her character will forever live on inside me. Alice Black is a fighter and so is her grandson. So to every person who gets in my way, to every person who wants to see me fail, to every person who says I can't do it, be warned! Alice Black's grandson is fighting mad and coming to get his just due!

12

When Tempers Flare

AFTER a couple of days of training camp, things were getting salty. I had aggravated my groin muscle to the point that it became inflamed. When the media saw that I wasn't practicing, it didn't take long for nasty rumors to start flying around. Nobody had the guts to say it in the open, but there was media speculation that I was faking the injury to try to force the Eagles to renegotiate. Here's how I found out about this.

I was lying on a table, getting treatment for what my doctor, Hank Sloan, diagnosed as *pubalgia,* which is technically *osteitis pubis*. Unfortunately, I am all too familiar with the medical terms. It's an inflammation of the tendons and muscles that attach the groin muscle to the pubic bone. It can be chronic, and flares up when I'm overworked. The problem is that because I condition myself year-round and hardcore, when coaches start training camp and try to get everyone into shape through two-a-day practices, I'm already in condition and can too easily aggravate my groin. I had a rough case of this over the years when I was with the 49ers.

After I went through two practices a day, the *pubalgia* acted up on me. If not treated properly, it could ruin my performance for the season. So I brought in Hank to go to work on me. We used hot laser treatment, which penetrates five inches into the body. The deep heat from the laser increases the blood flow and circulation through the tissue, activates the stem cells, and increases mitochondrial activity. This, along with the oxygen chamber, heals the injured cells and replenishes them with fresh oxygen. Those two processes are not bad; the injections are.

Hank's treatment session also involves two types of injections. He fills a syringe with a specifically designed mix of natural minerals, vitamins, and amino acids. He adjusts the formula for the different tissues he injects. There are two kinds of injections Hank does—one around the tendon to strengthen and grow the tissue, the other into muscle tissue to relax the muscle spasms and trigger points. The first type of injection involves prolotherapy, which involves a natural solution injection of dextrose, a sugar water solution, and procaine. Trigger points are bundles of muscle tissue within the larger muscle itself. The second injection relaxes the muscle fibers so they don't pull on the groin attachment. This injection has procaine, Traumeel, and vitamin B12. Overall, a typical treatment is six to ten injections in very specific places. The needles are small, but trust me—you feel them.

While I was going through that fun, would you believe the media had the nerve to accuse me of faking the injury? Coach Andy Reid knew better and responded to those rumors by saying: "It's a legitimate injury. This guy would never do that. He's not that type of guy. He would never go in that direction . . . I'm being cautious with it. I don't want it to get worse. It's a constant battle."

At that time, Andy Reid and I were hardly the best of friends. My problem with him was that he had the power to persuade Joe Banner that a compromise could be worked out, but he didn't want to. The only thing that mattered to me was that Andy Reid made the decision to go against me. I couldn't separate that decision from the person or the coach.

Still, I respected his honesty in telling the truth. He is an honest person. I like the person and respect the coach. There is nothing not to like about him: He is a good person, a great coach, and a man's man. Despite all of that, at the time I resented authority, and he was that authority.

I got the impression that some of the coaches were neither neutral nor in my corner. I felt uncomfortable around them and preferred not to interact with them unless it was business related. One of the coaches persisted in saying "Hi Terrell" in a manner that I took as antagonizing; I thought he was trying to irritate me. After a couple of days, I lost my patience, and told him not to talk to me unless I talked to him. Coach Reid did not like that at all, because that challenged his authority over the team.

Trouble was coming my way, and on August 10, the situation came to a head.

While the guys were practicing, I was directed by the head trainer to work on another field doing specific drills and exercises to rehabilitate my groin. It was hot outside, which made it more difficult to deal with a sore groin and not being able to practice to improve as a receiver.

At the end of practice, different players go over to an autograph area and sign items for the fans waiting after practice. For the second time it was supposed to be my turn to go over and sign autographs after that practice. One of the assistants came over to me and asked me to sign the autographs.

I had no problem with signing autographs, but I had just done my rehab exercises and I needed to get treatment on my groin as soon as possible after working it out. I didn't want everything to get cold. The trainers were expecting me.

Had I gone over to sign, the whole place would have run over to get my autograph. I was not being conceited about it, but I would have had to be there for an hour to sign the autographs for everybody. I don't like to sign for just a few minutes and leave: The kids who are next always get disappointed when I tell them I can't autograph their football, so I didn't want to do it.

With the first preseason game coming up in a few days, I wanted to do everything I could to get ready to play as soon as possible. So when I was asked to go sign the autographs, I said I wanted to go to my scheduled treatment instead.

Coach Reid didn't like that: He had a system that all of the players follow, and he told me to go over there and sign. I told him I was going to get my treatment. He lost his patience and told me, "Just shut up!"

I told him that I was a grown man and that he should shut up.

Coach Reid should not have told me to shut up, and I shouldn't have said that back to him. A part of me hated to get into a confrontation with him. Another part of me, the part that was just waiting for the chance to fight back against "the man," would not stand for that kind of disrespect. I wasn't going to accept being told to shut up by anyone. I hadn't raised my voice, cursed, or acted disrespectful to him in any way. I was frustrated. We both had tempers and egos.

We are both professionals, though. He ended the conversation and moved on. So did I. Despite all the anger inside me, no part of me wanted to get into a problem with him. I didn't like to see two good people with conflicting interests get into a bad situation.

I went to get treatment, and then took a shower, and on my way to the dorm room, Coach Reid's assistant called me on my cell phone and told me to go see him. I did so, and Coach Reid told me he was sending me home for a week to get things together, and to come back with a new attitude. I guess management thought that would make me feel contrite and fall in line. I didn't respond to the disciplinary action the way they wanted. It made me more determined to show the Eagles that I couldn't be broken no matter what they did.

They thought I would go home and come back with my tail between my legs. They thought wrong.

When the news broke that I was being sent home, the Philadelphia media went crazy. As I drove up the block toward my house, I called my publicist, Kim, because I saw the media already camped out around my house, waiting for me. The Eagles didn't say much about why I was sent home and neither did I. I pulled into my driveway and walked straight into my house.

There were fans there yelling for me to come out and sign autographs. Between the fans and the media, it was like a circus on my front lawn. After a couple of hours, I peeked out the window and saw a bunch of kids throwing a football around. I decided to go outside and have a little fun with them.

I signed autographs for everybody there, and then I started to shoot some hoops in my driveway. Reporters were shouting question after question. News helicopters were flying by, taking video footage of the scene.

After the media started asking why I wasn't in camp, I started doing some situps, and then pumped some iron. The crowd was counting each rep. They were having a ball.

As the questions kept coming about what had happened, I pretty much kept saying no comment. I was just having some fun. I wanted to show people that I wasn't crying and depressed. I wanted everybody to see me smiling and having a good time. The footage was everywhere on TV. All of America saw it.

After practice that day, Coach Reid said: "I did send him home. He's expected to return next Wednesday. It's in-house business and it's going to stay in-house. I'll work it out with TO. I'm not going to sit here and turn it into a bash session."

They wanted to keep their decision to send me home quiet. They wanted me to disappear and come back apologetic. They wanted to control me and the situation. It didn't exactly go down like that.

The next day, Kim, Drew, and Jason came to town. The media started speculating about what happened and I wanted to set the record straight. I couldn't hold my tongue anymore and agreed to do an interview on ESPN's *Pardon the Interruption* with Michael Wilbon and Bob Ryan. I also appeared live during halftime of ESPN's Thursday night NFL preseason football game between Green Bay and San Diego. They promoted the interview with Chris Berman during the game, and I doubt that many fans changed the channel at halftime.

The whole process so far had been very hard on me, and I didn't intend to keep quiet about it. I wanted to explain to America what was really going on. Somehow, the Eagles' perspective had been leaked to the press. The fans already had the Eagles' side of things, and they were about to get mine.

With Drew at my side, I told Ryan and Wilbon, "My attitude is not going to change. I came into training camp [and] was working toward being diligent and honoring my contract. I did that. As far as me going in and changing, nothing's going to change. I will not go out and try to be somebody I'm not."

When they asked me about my dispute with Coach Reid, I answered, "In the midst of that he told me to shut up. I just told him, I'm a grown man, and I told him the same, I told him to shut up. That was it. Everybody knows he's a controlling guy. He wants to be the main guy."

They brought up Donovan, and I spoke my mind, saying, "Everybody's calling me a hypocrite, [but] he's the same hypocrite. It was reported that he doesn't want to talk to me privately right now. Then I get to my dorm room, and he has his brother call a friend of mine to talk to me on the side. I have no desire to talk to Donovan."

When they asked me whether Donovan and I could play together, I answered, "I don't think so. I'm just being honest."

I went on national television and spoke the truth as I saw it. I no longer believed that I could work things out with Donovan and management, but I still felt we could be productive on the field and win games. I couldn't just sit back and take their punishment without dishing it right back at them. Whatever level our confrontation was on before, this took it to a whole new one. No owner, coach, or general manager wants to see a player get up on national television and tell it like it is. I called out the Eagles' management, coaches, and my quarterback on national television. This is just not done in the league.

Every expert commented that the situation had gone too far and had become unresolvable. They all thought that Donovan and I couldn't coexist on the field. They said that the Eagles were going to have to trade me.

How did the Eagles respond? The same way as before: There would be no renegotiation or trade. I could either play for my existing contract with the Eagles or not play at all. Once more, there would be no compromise.

As for Donovan, he responded by saying, "I still see no reason to talk. When we go on the field it's all about business. I can go the whole season without talking to him."

When it became clear that the Eagles were not going to trade me or renegotiate my contract, I realized that their priority was to maintain the system they had in place and not to set a precedent of compromising. Their system got them to three straight NFC Championship games before I got there. It was successful without me, but it was more successful with me in 2004. Unfortunately, I had gone from being that perfect missing piece last year to being a monkey wrench in the machine this year.

The Eagles played their first preseason game over the weekend while I stayed home. I could see that things were not going to work out this year, and there was nothing I could do to change that. I was going to have to play in a hostile atmosphere and risk injury. They were going to cut me after the season and move on. If I got hurt that season, I would never see another NFL paycheck again. My career was on the line and so was my faith.

I thought of my grandma and asked myself how she would want me to fight this fight from here. I knew she would want me to let my play on the field do the talking from then on. Game day would be my forum to state my case and show what I'm made of.

I made the decision to return Wednesday as a professional. No more disputes. No more confrontations. No more talking to the media. No more problems. I wanted to focus on playing the game of football that I love. I was going to do my job and leave it at that. I set my goal to leave business out of things and just concentrate on being the best wide receiver I could be. I didn't like some of the people around me, but I wasn't going to let that stop me from achieving my goal. I wasn't going to kiss butt and be a company man, but I was going to do my job. I was going to abide by my contract. When I returned to the Eagles' camp and stepped on that field, it was not to be the problem, but to be the answer.

13
Chemistry

WHEN I came back on Wednesday as scheduled, I minded my own business and did what was necessary. Donovan and I still didn't talk to each other. We were both too proud. I felt he owed me an apology and he felt the same. No one was willing to be the one to apologize first. There were a lot of strong wills around there.

The next preseason game was only a few days away. That wasn't enough time to get healthy, since my groin muscle was still inflamed. If it had been a regular-season game, I would have played, but the coaches knew it was not worth risking making the injury worse just to play in a preseason game.

The media were of course very critical of me, calling me a distraction and accusing me of ruining the team's chemistry. I'm going to set the record straight right now: Winning creates chemistry, not vice versa. Good position coaching, smart play calling, and good execution by competitive players create winning. The chemistry follows from the winning.

My first preseason game was Donovan's third. We were playing the Cincinnati Bengals. I felt that the world wanted to see me drop passes, get covered and shut down; they were anxiously waiting to point the finger at me and say, "I told you so!"

They just couldn't wait to blame me for everything wrong in the world.

But when I ran onto the field, I could tell that a lot of the fans were still with me. They were mad, but I knew I could win them over. There were some boos and cheers as they called my name. The 81 jerseys were still in the stands.

I admit most preseason games are no big deal. Typically, I just want to get some basic work in with respect to the timing with my quarterback and then get out of the game. I especially hate to see players get injured in the preseason, because the games are meaningless. Starters just try to get in, have some quick success, then get out.

This game was different. I had something to prove. The experts said I could not be successful on the field because of my actions off the field. I felt I could be dominant regardless of the situation with the Eagles. I was hungry to back up my words and to prove everybody wrong. I was eager to make something happen.

I had felt nothing but frustration and disappointment for the last several months. This was my chance to win. This was my chance to vent all that negativity that I had endured. This was my chance to compete. I wanted satisfaction.

On the very first play of the game, I lined up across from Pro Bowl cornerback Deltha O'Neal. He was in my way. That was his job. I had my job to do as well, but this was now more than business. This was personal—not against him, but against all the haters out there.

I waited for the center to snap the ball and made my move. I sidestepped O'Neal and took off. I ran by him and streaked down the right sideline wide open. Donovan saw me and hit me right in stride for a sixty-four-yard touchdown.

"Yes! That's right!" I screamed. The crowd went crazy cheering for me. I loved it and they still loved me. That felt good, real good.

When we got the ball again, Donovan came right back to me. I caught another pass and ran with it, taking the ball thirty-one yards downfield to their twenty-eight yard line. In our first two drives, I had two catches for ninety-five yards.

I only played the first half, but I still had five catches for 131 yards with one touchdown. I was as good as ever.

There was justice in the world again, at least in my world. It would have been easy for me to talk to the media and gloat after a performance like that, but I didn't trust them; I knew they would find some way to take what I said and make it controversial. I didn't want any more problems. I was going to do my job and that was that. I wasn't going to be happy, but I was going to play my best and help this team win.

The next week was the last game of the preseason, which is always the least significant. The most important game is the third week, which made my performance even more satisfying. The third preseason game is when the starters play the most, sometimes as much as the first three quarters. The coaches put together a specific game plan designed to attack the opponent's weaknesses for that game, and it's a good indication of how the team is progressing. The coaches don't bother to put in a game plan for the fourth game, and the starters usually don't play for more than the first quarter. Donovan and I both sat out the game. He watched from a skybox and I was on the sidelines. The Eagles lost, but no one gave it a thought. All the talk was about the season opener versus the Atlanta Falcons.

This game was a rematch of last year's NFC Championship Game, and most experts predicted it would be a preview of this year's NFC Championship Game as well. The Eagles and the Falcons were widely considered to be the two best teams in the NFC. I don't remember too many people predicting the Seahawks or the Panthers would be there.

The game was also the *Monday Night Football* regular-season debut. It was a game that people had circled on their calendar months before. We were all fired up about it and I was ready to play. It didn't matter that I had almost no communication with my coaches (except for my wide receiver coach) and hadn't talked with Donovan. There was an understanding that we were all going to work together. I still wanted a new deal, but the only thing I could do to help myself was to play excellent football and hope to not get hurt.

Now that the season was starting, I had three objectives: be the best receiver in the league, stay healthy, and lead this team to a Super Bowl victory. Getting a new contract was no longer part of my game plan. I told myself not to worry about things I could not control and to just focus on my three objectives.

Leading into the game, I agreed to do a couple of interviews. The number-one thing everybody wanted to know was how I felt about Donovan. As usual, I spoke my mind, and said the following to ESPN's Michael Irvin: "It's not that I hate Donovan. I love Donovan. I don't hate him at all. I was disappointed in a few things. I have the right to do that. Everyone speaks out of emotion. Everybody speaks out of frustration. Everybody's done it. That means I'm human. If you want me to go in and say I was wrong, maybe I was. Maybe I wasn't."

Of course, the media cherry-picked what I had to say and focused on my "I love Donovan" statement. They called me enigmatic. Look, I did have love for Donovan, and a part of me still does. I viewed Donovan as a friend, until he got confrontational with me in the locker room rather than apologize for insulting me. After that, I became very angry with him for turning on me. Nevertheless, the Donovan I knew before that was one of the most likable guys I ever met.

When I was asked if I would communicate with Donovan, I answered, "I will. You guys will see. It's not going to be a year-long thing. Leading up to this Monday night game, things will get worked out."

First of all, I did not attack him; that was not my intent. Second, I had a reason for being angry with him, but nobody knew that. Third, because I wouldn't talk about what happened in our locker room, public opinion turned against me. Fourth, people questioned my character when I was acting because of a principle rather than out of concern for my popularity. And fifth, I am telling the story now only because Donovan already let the cat out of the bag and talked.

So when the media asked me about my contract situation, I told them, "It'll get resolved one way or another. Right now, we'll put the contract situation on the shelf, but after we win the Super Bowl, it'll get revisited."

As far as everything else was concerned, I made it clear to the media that I had put my problems with the Eagles behind me and was focusing on the game against the Falcons.

The tough thing about *Monday Night Football* games is the long wait to play. The anticipation builds and builds all day. With one o'clock games, the action starts early in the day; with nine o'clock games, you've got eight more hours of idle time. It's easy to get overly nervous or anxious. I handle it by keeping busy, listening to my iPod, and staying loose.

By the time we took the field, tensions were high and it showed. We were on the road facing a loud, hostile crowd in Atlanta. Both squads were hyped up to the max. When we both took the field before kickoff, the players started taunting each other and exchanging insults. One thing led to another and players started pushing and shoving. Kevin Mathis, a backup cornerback for the Falcons, threw a punch at the Eagles' Pro Bowl linebacker Jeremiah Trotter, one of the leaders of the team. Every player and coach on that Eagles team, and I mean every single one of them without exception, had nothing but the ultimate respect for Jeremiah.

Jeremiah responded by attempting to block the guy's punch, accidentally striking his face mask. Unfortunately, that reaction was somehow enough for the officials to eject Jeremiah as well as Mathis from the game. That wasn't exactly an even exchange. Trotter is the most valuable player on that defense because of his leadership and experience. No disrespect to the other great players on the defense, such as Jevon Kearse, but Trotter runs the defense, and it was the defense that got this team to the NFC Championship four years in a row. It was the defense that put our offense in position to win the Super Bowl.

It hurt to lose Jeremiah. That wasn't how we wanted to start the game. The offense knew we had to step up.

We got the ball first and instantly drew a penalty against the Falcons, giving us the ball on our forty-nine yard line. The next play, Donovan threw my way and we gained fifteen yards. He went to me again a couple of plays later but we misfired. Our kicker missed a field goal try and the Falcons got the ball.

With Jeremiah gone, the Falcons ran the ball all over our defense. Fortunately, they called a passing play and we were able to pick the ball off.

We took the field deep in our own territory, at the eighteen yard line. Donovan hit me for a quick four-yard gain on the sideline. He went to me again, but this time he threw an interception.

The Eagles' defense kept the Falcons from scoring, and we got another shot at it. Donovan threw a couple of incomplete passes and we had to punt. We weren't off to a great offensive start by any means.

This time, the Falcons drove the ball down the field and scored off a seven-yard run by Falcons quarterback Michael Vick, taking a 7–0 first-quarter lead.

We went three and out and had to punt. The Falcons got

the ball back and scored again to take a 14–0 lead in the first quarter.

The defense held them from there for the rest of the game. It was time for the offense to do our part. With the pressure on, Donovan and I connected for a fourteen-yard gain and then again for sixteen yards. From there, we ran the ball and threw it to Westbrook for a touchdown to make it 14–7 in the second quarter.

Both teams went back and forth, and we got the ball on our thirty-five with a little over two minutes to go. This was our chance to tie the game before the end of the half. On the first play, Donovan hit me for fifteen yards to midfield. From there, we moved the ball into field-goal range, but David Akers missed another kick.

The defense remained strong at the start of the third quarter and got us the ball back at our twenty-five yard line. We moved it a little, and then I caught a twenty-three-yard pass to put us in scoring position at the Falcons' three yard line. Unfortunately, on the next play, while Donovan dropped back and looked downfield, he took a hard hit and fumbled, and Atlanta recovered.

The rest of the third quarter, Donovan didn't look my way. On offense, we were forced to punt and had another quarterback fumble. In the fourth quarter, down 14–7, on third down deep in our own territory, we were in a tough spot. Needing to make something happen, I got open, caught the ball, and gained nineteen yards to get us downfield. A couple of plays later, we were in field-goal position, and this time Akers made the kick to bring us within four points.

From there, Donovan and I had a hard time connecting, and we found ourselves in a bad spot with 1:38 to go in the game, fourth down and ten yards. This was our last chance to win the game. It was all on the line.

The Falcons knew I was the guy to stop. Donovan knew I

was the guy to go to. Donovan took the snap from shotgun formation and looked my way. I had to get ten yards for the first down to keep us in the game. I was thinking I could do better. So was Coach Reid, who called for me to go deep. I made my move, got separation, and sprinted open down the sideline. I could feel that I was gonna make the play and win the game. My adrenaline was pumping as I turned back for the ball and saw it fall way too short for me to have a chance at it. Donovan got hit by a defensive lineman as he threw the ball and couldn't get his strength into the pass.

I knew that if I didn't put up some serious numbers, the media would come after me. I caught seven passes for 112 yards, so the critics couldn't be negative about my performance.

That I'd made a positive contribution didn't mean I wanted to talk to the media. I wasn't going to give them a chance to twist my comments into something controversial. I wasn't trying to be a problem for the Eagles, so I flew low on the radar screen, didn't comment, and got out of there.

During the game, the camera caught Donovan and me speaking briefly to each other about what was going on in the game. The media tried to make that into a big thing, but it wasn't. We were talking, which was a start, but that was all it was.

Donovan said to the media, "I guess that's something positive for you guys to talk about. . . . We could have been talking about food in the vending machines."

I felt good about it, because our brief conversation about the game was an improvement. I wanted things to get better. I wanted to put in my time, have a good year, win the Super Bowl, stay healthy, and get a new contract either with the Eagles or through free agency. I hoped that was how things would work out. Man, was I naïve!

The second game of the season was something I'd been looking forward to for a long time, since we were playing the

San Francisco 49ers. We were at home, coming off a tough loss, and we were hungry for a win.

It's never a fun week of practice after a loss, but I was psyched, since I'd never played against a former team before. Some of the defensive players on the 49ers made negative comments about me, which gave me a little extra motivation. Also, it was my first home game of the regular season, and I wanted to put on a show for the fans who stuck by me.

On the first play of the game, Donovan threw a short, four-yard pass to our tight end. Then he threw an incompletion on second down. On third and six at our thirty-two yard line, it was time to come to me; Donovan dropped back and did a good job of scrambling around and buying time for himself until he saw me running across the middle. I caught the ball twenty-eight yards downfield and took off, running another forty yards to score the game's opening touchdown.

The crowd went crazy! I'd scored on the third play of the game. It felt great, and to make things even better, I turned around, ran toward Donovan, and exchanged a low-five with him. We were both happy and walked to the sideline to-gether. As wild as the crowd was when I crossed the goal line, they were even more out of control after that!

The defense, with Jeremiah Trotter back in the lineup, stopped the 49ers and gave us the ball back. We were unable to move the ball and had to punt.

On the next series, Donovan threw me a twenty-yard pass at midfield. I was hit hard but hung on to the ball. The de-fender, Mike Rumph, wanted to stand over me and talk trash, hoping I would lie down and roll over, but that didn't hap-pen. It was an ESPN highlight hit, but I jumped right up and ran back to the huddle as if it had never happened. I knew that Rumph and the entire defense were shocked that I got up immediately. Sometimes my opponents forget that I'm not just fast and elusive, but also strong and tough.

Something happened to the defense after that hit. At first,

they were all fired up like they had taught me a lesson. All that changed the moment I stood up and jogged back to the huddle. Like air coming out of a tire, when they saw me take their best shot and come back for more, their momentum slipped through their grasp.

Three plays later, I caught another short pass and moved the ball to the San Fran twenty-eight yard line. Two plays later, Donovan threw a short touchdown to our tight end.

The defense held the 49ers' offense in check, and on our next possession I had a short catch that ultimately led to a missed field goal.

Early in the second quarter, on third and seven, we were up 14–0 with the ball on our forty-two yard line. It was still a competitive game, but it was time to take over. Donovan took the snap and threw it to me deep. I caught the ball around the fifteen yard line and ran it in for the score.

The crowd cheered as I stood in the end zone, nodded, and stared at the crowd. I soaked in the satisfaction of the moment and then went to Donovan and handed him the ball. That was my second gesture to try to bridge the gap between us. It wasn't an apology, but it was a sign of good faith.

After just nineteen minutes of play, I had 143 yards and two touchdowns on five catches. Imagine what I could have done if I had played the remaining forty-one minutes! With a big lead and with me still banged up a bit, the coaches decided that I should sit out the rest of the game. As long as we kept command, I didn't mind staying out of harm's way.

We ended up winning 42–3. After the game, I again didn't talk to the media. I was happy with the win and my performance and I'd stayed healthy. I didn't see the point of saying anything that the media could twist into something controversial.

Andy Reid, who calls it like he sees it, was asked about the 49ers' talking trash about me during the week. He answered, "He didn't let all of that bother him. I'm sure everybody has their opinion on him on that team. Some guys like him and some don't, but he goes through that every week. Guys taunt him, but he doesn't get into that."

Coach Reid was right. I don't let the defensive backs get in my head with their insults. I don't let them stop me from reaching my goals.

In response to the positive gestures I made, Donovan said to the media, "Whatever happened in the past, hopefully it's over. . . . When we're in the field and everything is clicking, everyone is smiling."

Although I made those attempts on the field, he never did anything to try to reconcile things off the field. To be fair, neither did I. Don't get me wrong, we both wanted to win, more than anything, and on game day, we'd do whatever was necessary. It was between Sundays that we couldn't let go of our grievances with each other. It was a battle of wills, when it should have been water under the bridge.

Nothing significant happened during the week of preparation for our next game, at home against the Oakland Raiders.

Not much happened with our offense either in the first half of that game, and we went into the half losing 10–6. I had only two catches for twenty yards. The game had the added attraction of me versus Raider wide receiver Randy Moss.

The game plan was for us to come out and start the third quarter by getting me the ball. After throwing some short passes and running the ball, we'd gotten to the Raider nineteen yard line. On first and ten, I caught a ten-yard pass to the nine yard line. On the next play, Donovan threw to me again for five yards. On the next play I scored a touchdown off a four-yard throw to take a 13–10 lead.

After punting on our next possession, we moved the ball down the field again. Late in the third I caught a pass for nine yards to get to the Raider five yard line. On the next play, we scored to make it 20–10.

The Raiders came back and got a field goal at the start of

the fourth quarter. Our next two drives were unsuccessful, and Oakland took advantage by scoring a touchdown to tie the game late in the fourth quarter.

With 2:17 to go, we had the ball on our twenty yard line. We needed a field goal to win. Our problem was that David Akers had injured his hamstring on the opening kickoff and could only kick an extremely short field goal. Normally we'd need to get to the thirty yard line or so to be in field-goal range, but with Akers in such bad shape, we had to get to the five yard line or so for him to have any chance of making the kick.

We threw short passes to dink and dunk our way down to the Raider forty-six yard line, but by then the clock had ticked down to only fifty-six seconds. We had a ten-yard penalty, which put us in a first and twenty situation. Dinking and dunking wasn't going to work any more, there wasn't enough time, so Coach Reid called my number: Donovan threw it to me and I moved the ball fifteen yards to the Raider thirty-one yard line. That would usually be enough, but with Akers's hurt leg, we had to get a lot closer.

The next play was an incompletion to another receiver that stopped the clock with forty seconds left. On third and five at the Raider thirty-one, Coach Reid and Donovan went to me again. This time the play went for fourteen yards to the Raider seventeen yard line. That still was not close enough.

Donovan threw an incompletion on the next play, which at least stopped the clock. The play also drew a five-yard penalty on Oakland, moving the ball to the twelve yard line with twenty-five seconds to go, and no time-outs left. Coach Reid called my number again, and I caught another pass to bring the ball to the five yard line. That was finally close enough, and after Donovan spiked the ball to stop the clock, Akers made the kick for the win.

My final stats were nine catches for eighty yards and a touchdown.

Our next game, against the Kansas City Chiefs, was even crazier. It was our fourth game, and by this time Donovan had been hit with various injuries, including a strained abdominal groin muscle, commonly known as a sports hernia.

Midway through the second quarter, we were down 17–0, and Donovan was having a tough time. We caught a break when our secondary picked off a pass and returned it for a touchdown, bringing the score to 17–6. We went for two points and missed. Then we kicked off and the Chiefs returned the kick for a touchdown, going up on us 24–6.

We found ourselves at midfield losing by eighteen points with 2:40 to go before the half. On second and ten, Donovan threw my way. The pass was incomplete but drew a penalty, giving us five yards and a first down. A couple of plays later, it was first and ten again on the thirty-five with 1:30 left. If we were to have any chance to come back, it had to be on this drive. A field goal was not going to get it done and Donovan couldn't just dump it off to the running back. We had to challenge the secondary down the field and everybody, including the Chiefs, knew it was time for me to make something happen.

Sure enough, Donovan went to me and I took the ball twenty-eight yards downfield, and on the next play I scored on a seven-yard touchdown pass. We went into the half trailing 24–13. We were back in the game.

From there, Donovan got in a rhythm and we were on fire. Overall, I caught eleven passes for 171 yards and one touchdown as we won the game 37–31.

After four games, we were 3–1. We were in position to make a run at winning the NFC East and the whole conference again. At that point, I had caught thirty-two passes for 506 yards and four touchdowns. Despite all the controversy

in the off-season and training camp, I was having a more productive year thus far than I had the year before.

I was putting together a tremendous season and I communicated with my quarterback and coaches on the field as required. I was honoring my word by coming in and giving my
best effort to help us win football games on Sundays.

Up next was the Cowboys game, and all seemed well in
Philly. In the far distance, though, the clouds were gathering
and the skies above were starting to darken, as the oncoming
storm was heading straight toward Philly.

14

The Calm Before the Storm

AFTER getting off to such a strong start, the offense really struggled after the first quarter of the season. It was no secret that Donovan was suffering from injuries to his abdomen, chest, and groin; he wasn't healthy, and it showed. Against Dallas, we were down 17–0 in the first quarter. They put up two touchdowns and a field goal before we could even get a first down.

Unlike the week before when we got hot and came back, we couldn't get anything going. We lost, 33–10. Our only touchdown came off the return of a Keyshawn Johnson fumble. The loss was downright ugly. There would be no touchdown celebrations on the Cowboys' star logo for me that day.

However, instead of doing something that angered Cowboy fans, I actually paid tribute to my friend Michael Irvin. Michael is one of the greatest receivers and Cowboys to ever play the game. He was called "The Playmaker" with good reason; he was something special during the Cowboys' Super Bowl run in the 1990s.

Not only was he special on the field, but he's a very special person off the field. Everybody who knows Michael absolutely loves him. No one on the planet has a more charismatic, likable personality than Michael. Over the years, I developed a friendship with him. During the difficult off-season I'd endured, Michael was the only football commentator with the guts to support my point of view. When it was unpopular and politically incorrect, Michael said the Eagles should either pay me or trade me. He took on all the media out there trying to appease popular opinion and stuck by me. While he didn't agree with everything I did, he wasn't afraid to tell the world that I had a valid point, too. He had the guts to tell it like he saw it; he also had the guts to tell me how he saw it. I have a lot of respect for him, and I decided to honor him by wearing his old throwback Cowboy jersey to the game.

Coach Reid had a dress code for the team, prohibiting the guys from dressing casually in jeans and sneakers to the game. I, along with several other players, sometimes didn't follow the rule.

The media made a big deal about it, as if I'd put on the jersey after the game because we lost. Little did they know that I came to Texas Stadium before the game wearing the Cowboys' number 88. If we had won, it wouldn't have been a big deal, but because we lost, the media were hoping Coach Reid would get angry and a new controversy would pop up for them to write about.

Coach Reid didn't see it that way. He actually stood up for me, saying, "He's a big Michael Irvin fan. On the way home, I give these guys an opportunity to wear comfortable clothes. I have done that since I have been here, and he's very close with Michael. I don't think it's that big of a deal."

There it was: Coach Reid said he didn't think it was a big deal, much to the media's disappointment. I meant no disrespect to anyone in wearing that jersey; I wore it to show respect for my friend. I don't see anything wrong with that and evidently neither did Coach Reid.

We had a bye week after the loss. When you lose, it usually

helps to have another game to look forward to as a way of re-bounding. It wasn't fun to head into a bye week after a loss, but we had a lot of players who were pretty banged up and needed the week to try to get healthy.

Our next game was at home, against the San Diego Charg-ers. Even with a week's rest, our offense was still off-track. I caught the offense's only touchdown of the last two games, a four-yard reception with about five minutes to go in the first half that gave us a 7–0 lead.

On one level, it was just a touchdown in a midseason game. But to me it was something special, because it was my one hundredth career touchdown reception. My girlfriend Felisha, friends from Chicago, Drew, Robert, and Kim were all there to witness this accomplishment. I was only the sixth player in the history of the NFL to catch one hundred touch-down passes. That's the kind of achievement that makes a player worthy of the Hall of Fame.

When a player in this league reaches a milestone like that, he's usually recognized during the game, especially when the achievement comes at the player's home field. To honor the player, an announcement is made on the scoreboard and over the public-address system. The whole thing charges up the crowd, creates goodwill for the player with his team-mates, the organization, the fans, and the community, and can also be a momentum-builder during the game. This would have been a great opportunity for me to further bond with the fans.

When I scored that hundredth career touchdown recep-tion, I celebrated by pulling out a towel, wiping down the ball, folding the towel over my arm, and walking away hold-ing the ball up to the crowd as if I were a waiter serving a dish. It was original and fun to do. My teammates seemed to enjoy it.

As I walked back to the sideline, I looked up at the scoreboard to see the milestone acknowledged on the big screen. I didn't see anything. I listened to the announcer but heard no announcement. The Eagles didn't do anything to celebrate my accomplishment. I would have been happy with any type of statement so the crowd could enjoy the moment with me, but apparently that was too much to ask.

I'd done everything asked of me since the start of the season to perform at the highest level and help this team be successful. I was doing my best and delivering. I had taken a beating all year long without complaint. I knew my actions in the off-season weren't going to be popular and I accepted that. However, when I accomplished something very special, something positive for the organization, I expected some acknowledgment, or at least to be recognized in front of the fans so they could decide whether to congratulate me. I was disappointed, and I took it as a slap in the face.

The game turned out to be a wild one with a crazy finish. Things were looking pretty tough for us late in the fourth quarter when the Chargers lined up to kick a field goal. They were winning 17–13, looking to increase their lead to seven when Quintin Mickell blocked the kick and Matt Ware picked it up and went sixty-five yards to give us the lead and the win, 20–17.

A win is a win, no matter what. We were happy to walk away from that one on top, but it was obvious our offense was struggling.

After the game and during the next week, I found it hard to let go of my disappointment at how the Eagles had ignored my TD. Still, I was determined to focus on getting through the season as best I could. Next on the list was a tough road game against the Denver Broncos. That game was especially tough for me because I would be going against cornerback Champ Bailey, whom many consider the top corner in the game.

The week of the Broncos game, Coach Reid addressed the team about wearing professional attire at away games. When we were winning, the dress code was not an issue, but after losing to the Cowboys, the coaching staff was looking to tighten the reins a little bit. Keeping things light, on the plane ride to Denver I wore a tuxedo with sneakers. The whole team, even the coaches, thought it was funny.

Leading up to the game, the media wanted me to comment on the matchup between Champ and me. I didn't talk to the media about it; Champ, however, said this about me before the game: "He can be a sleeper. . . . Sometimes, he may not do anything for a couple of series and then he explodes, and before you know it he has his six catches for 120 yards. He's going to make his plays. But you just have to be there to stop him, and I'm ready for it . . . I'm ready for him."

The Broncos were definitely ready for us; they jumped all over us from the beginning. They took a 28–0 lead in the second quarter. We went in at the half losing 28–7.

Despite our bleak situation, I still believed we could win the game. With ten minutes to go in the third quarter, I was determined to make something happen. On second and twelve, Donovan threw me a very short pass for about four yards. Champ Bailey was playing a couple of yards off me, one on one without help. As soon as I caught the ball, I turned upfield and he was waiting for me. For a moment we stood face to face, man to man.

I took a quick step to the outside, as I was near the right sideline. The moment he jumped outside with me, I cut inside, swatted his arms away, and raced down the sideline. He got knocked off-balance and couldn't catch up as I turned on the jets, outrunning the other defenders trying to get me. The play went for a ninety-one-yard touchdown. That was the longest play of my career and of Donovan's. The crowd was stunned and we had new life.

Our defense stopped the Broncos twice and gave us another chance with 4:24 left in the third quarter. We had the ball on our own thirty-one yard line. After we gained five yards on a running play, Coach Reid called my number on second down. Once more, I made a big play to beat Champ Bailey, for forty-six yards. This set up a touchdown and brought us back to within seven points.

We were back in the game. The defense held strong once again. We started the fourth quarter with good field position and marched down to the Bronco twenty-four yard line. Unfortunately, we threw an interception and lost the momentum.

After the interception, the Broncos scored three straight touchdowns to beat us 49–21. I had three catches for 154 yards and the one touchdown. Little did I know that the ninety-one yard touchdown would be my last as a Philadelphia Eagle.

Once again, after the game I didn't talk to the media. I wasn't happy about losing that game, but I bit my tongue and stayed quiet. The late-night flight home from Denver to Philly was a smooth ride. It was the last period of calm before the storm.

After each game of the 2005 season, I would put on my headphones, play my iPod, and walk out of the locker room without answering questions from the media. I didn't want to talk to the Philadelphia reporters because I knew they were looking for controversy.

I didn't want any trouble with the press or the Eagles. I had my share of fun here and there, but for the most part, there were no noticeable incidents that the Eagles could fairly point to as problematic. I'd kept my word when I returned to training camp that I would give the Eagles organization my best effort to help get back to the Super Bowl. But I guess that's not the kind of thing the press likes to write about.

I had agreed to do an interview with Michael Irvin during the season because he never took any cheap shots at me on camera. Everything he said about me on the air, he also said to my face. He was honest with me and didn't sell me out to garner favor with his boss or public opinion.

The only other public comments I made were on a weekly ESPN radio show for a few minutes every Thursday.

I stuck to those two interview formats the entire season, until I got a request from my friend Graham Bensinger, a nineteen-year-old freshman at Syracuse University who's studying to become a broadcast journalist. I had gotten to know Graham when he was a high-school student back in San Francisco; he had a weekly radio show and I talked to him from time to time on his show to help him out.

Graham contacted me and told me that ESPN.com would hire him to do an interview with me in my home. He asked me to do him a favor. He said it would be a soft, positive piece that was supposed to appear on the Internet at ESPN.com. After putting it off, I agreed to help him out. Not too many college freshmen get to do an interview for ESPN.com with a premier sports personality. We set it up for Thursday, November 3.

When I awoke on Thursday, I never dreamed this day would be the beginning of the end of my career as a Philadelphia Eagle.

From the look of my ankle, the day was starting out ominously. During that Bronco game, I'd reinjured my ankle, the same one that I had rehabilitated to get back to the Super Bowl. I twisted it during the game and it swelled up pretty bad. I'd aggravated the ligaments where the pins and plate had been inserted. It blew up on me the next morning, and it looked so bad, the Eagles listed me as doubtful to play the upcoming game versus the Washington Redskins. Nevertheless, I felt that with proper treatment from trainer Rick Burkholder, I could tough it out and play.

When asked about my injury, Coach Reid told the media, "He is hurting. . . . He is sore. It's going to be a fight to get him there for Sunday. We're taking it day by day. He's made progress the last couple of days."

I was making progress because I was working extremely hard around the clock between my work with Rick and my oxygen chamber. It was not fun, but my fun comes on Sundays and I desperately wanted to play in that game.

On Thursday morning, I went into the training room to work with Rick. He applied electrical stimulation to maximize the blood flow in my ankle, and then I soaked my foot in the cold whirlpool.

Rick was in the room with me when all of a sudden I heard a lot of yelling. I saw Hugh Douglas walk into the room and scream profanities at me. The training room is close enough to the locker room to allow one to hear any commotion from either room.

Hugh came in and, looking to start a fight, accused me of faking my injury. Hugh had played defensive end for the Eagles for many years, but was cut in the preseason. He was still around because Andy Reid loves Hugh Douglas. Hugh is one of Coach Reid's all-time favorite guys. Hugh had been a team leader and always had a strong presence in the locker room. When Hugh couldn't play for Coach Reid anymore, he gave Hugh a job titled "Team Ambassador." Coach Reid wanted Hugh to be around the guys and to have a presence as an Eagle in the community.

In any event, Hugh and I had some bad blood between us. When I was seeking a new contract in the off-season, Hugh was the only guy outside of Donovan who spoke against me to the media. I didn't appreciate that. When I showed up for training camp, Hugh tried to apologize and smooth things over. That he apologized didn't mean I had to accept it. I didn't like what he had said about me and I didn't want to be his friend. I wasn't looking to be his enemy, either; I never bothered him or insulted him, but I wasn't going to befriend him. Hugh took that as an insult and had it in for me.

As if I didn't have enough problems with my ankle, I now had a big defensive end weighing fifty pounds more than me, looking to get me. Hugh wouldn't stop yelling out insults and accusations that I was faking my injuries. After talking trash in the training room, he started saying the same stuff to all the guys in the locker room. Just about everybody was there. He called me out in front of everyone and challenged my manhood. I'd had enough.

Hugh wanted to fight because of rumors going around in the media that I was faking it. All the guys knew by the size of my ankle and by what Rick had to say to the coaches that I had a bad ankle sprain. I had nearly killed myself trying to get ready to practice that day, and this guy was accusing me of faking an injury.

Other than stealing from other guys in the locker room, faking an injury is about the worst thing a player can do to his teammates. After all the painful, hard work I had gone through, for this guy to go around saying I was this and that was more than I could stand for. I didn't care that he was part of management now; no one was going to get away with all this talk—not without a fight.

Ready to stand my ground, I got out of the whirlpool, put on my slippers to have some solid footing, and walked into the locker room where Hugh was still talking trash. I went up to him, stood face to face, and talked back to him.

Hugh was fuming and lost his temper. So did I.

In slow motion, we looked into each other's eyes and knew it was going down. He threw a right hook toward my face. It was coming hard and fast, but I was quick enough to duck under it. Although I got low, his fist still grazed the top of my head. I hit him in the body but he grabbed me. We exchanged blows, but we were being pulled apart before either of us could connect a solid punch.

I broke free of his grasp and saw the whole team there watching. I stood in front of the whole team and furiously challenged anyone else who wanted a piece of me.

I stood up to Hugh, and I fought him. Hugh knew that what he did was wrong. It was humiliating to be called those names and be accused of faking an injury in front of my teammates. It was even worse to have to get into a fight, and it was rock bottom to have to challenge anyone else who had a problem with me.

Did I run to Coach Reid and tell him what the Team Ambassador did? Did I complain to management? Did I complain to my agents or my publicist? Did I complain to the NFLPA? Did I file a lawsuit against the Eagles for what management said and did?

No. I didn't tell anyone. What happens in the locker room is supposed to stay inside the locker room. I took what happened like a man and carried my burden.

Hugh immediately went to see Coach Reid to tell him what had happened. Did Coach Reid say anything to me? Did Coach Reid ask me what happened? Did he or anyone else from the Eagles' management apologize to me?

No. If it had been any other player who had been assaulted like that, the Eagles' front office would have apologized to that player and disciplined Hugh. But management didn't care that I was attacked like that. I knew I wasn't among friends on this team. I didn't cry about it or let anyone know that it bothered me.

I wasn't going to let anyone think that they got the best of me. So I practiced that day and did what I had to do.

After practice, the media had no clue about what had happened in the locker room. They thought it was newsworthy that I practiced. Little did they know what really went down. Coach Reid obviously didn't let the media know what happened; when he was asked about how I did at practice, all he said was, "He did a nice job. . . . We limited his reps, but he did a nice job when he was in there. It's a matter of getting the swelling out. We'll see where it's at tomorrow."

My ankle hurt during practice and was sore afterward. I was having a bad day and I wasn't in the best of moods. I was not happy to have to do the interview with Graham Bensinger, but I didn't have the heart to cancel on him. This interview meant everything to him, so I kept my word and did the interview.

If I thought that was a bad day, little did I know what was coming next.

15
The Interview

IF I hadn't been promising the kid that I would give him his big interview for the last couple of weeks, I would have postponed it. I should have, I wish I had, but I thought it was the right thing to keep my word. Graham Bensinger was a good kid and this was his big break, so I thought it best to just tough it out and take an hour to help him out. I figured after that I could go to sleep and put the rough day behind me.

It was supposed to be just an Internet interview, but he showed up with a TV camera. I didn't make a big deal out of it. We set it up to do the interview in my study room.

We talked for fifty-seven minutes. Here are some key parts:

Graham Bensinger: I've known you for a few years now. I can see [the strain] in your face. I could see it in the off-season, and I can see it now. Are you happy?

Terrell Owens: Yeah, I mean, right now, there have been some ups and downs. But overall, I think the things that have gone on, I put them in the back of my mind. I've put those things on the shelf, and when I go out there on the field, I try to have fun. But, yeah, overall, I would say that I'm pretty happy.

GB: You seem to have gone from enjoying the media attention, the hype, the craze, to completely secluding yourself
from it. Why?

TO: Well, it's almost like I'm in a no-win situation with the
media sometimes. . . . You know, I know how the media is. I
know how TV works. They'll throw a question out there and
they'll edit it. You know, the way they want to put it out there
to the world. So, my thing is just to let my play do the talking
for me, and that has been my stance this year.

Here I was saying that the media edits what I say and
displays it out of context. Unfortunately, I was extremely pro-
phetic about this.

GB: If the Eagles win and you don't rack up the numbers statistically, are you satisfied?

TO: Yeah, I mean, that's the name of the game. Honestly, it's
wins and losses when it all boils down to it. And that's how I
look at it. I always said that, even when I was in San Francisco.
I just said as long as we're winning, I don't have a problem
with it. But if we're not winning and I'm not getting the ball
enough, that's when I have a problem. Because it doesn't matter statistically. I feel like with me being a big part of any offense, then the numbers are going to come. . . . I think at some
point during the course of the game, I will have an impact—
whether it's blocking or whether it's catching the football.

Okay, could I possibly have been more of a team player
than that? I said that I wanted the Eagles to win more than I
wanted to put up big numbers.

GB: Has there been something [you've] said or done over the
past year that you regret?

TO: No, not at all. I think the thing is, I know deep down inside that I've always been honest, and I've been truthful about the things that I've said. Like the saying goes, sometimes the truth hurts. And, a lot of people don't like to hear the truth. So, as long as I'm honest with myself, I can live with it.

The truth hurts, all right. Little did I know that speaking the truth would end my career with the Eagles.

GB: You just said that following the Super Bowl, you obviously said that you weren't the only one, or you weren't the one that got tired, in referring to Donovan McNabb. Do you think your honesty becomes detrimental at times?

TO: No, not at all. I think with that comment, I said it probably in regards to my own conditions because I hadn't practiced with the team since my injury. I never referred to Donovan in that comment. A lot of people speculated, and they just assumed that I was talking about Donovan. That's not what I mean, and that's not what I meant. A lot of people take a lot of things that I say out of context. If I didn't say his name in particular, then I wasn't talking about him.

As I explained before, I was responding to the media's attack on my work ethic and conditioning. I was talking about myself, not Donovan. We went on from there.

GB: You've never won a championship at any level. Not in high school, not in college, not yet in the NFL. What was it like to be that close against the Patriots?

TO: It was an interesting feeling. It was very exciting, you know. After it was over, it was just, you know. . . . After playing nine years in the league, some guys have played this game all their life, and they've never gotten to that point. So, I didn't take it for granted. . . . Whatever I could do, I left it on the field. I played hard. We just came up short. I think there are opportunities that we had to win the ballgame, and you know, we played a great team, and a great team beat us. I don't feel like it was a cakewalk [for New England]. We took it to the wire with them.

Although we lost, we played well as a team.

GB: You just recently scored your one hundredth career receiving touchdown, which puts you in remarkably elite company with only you and Marvin Harrison as the two active players to have accomplished the feat. What does it mean for you?

TO: I didn't really think too much of it. Obviously, it's a great accomplishment. I guess if I look down the road some time, I'll look back on it and and see how special it is. But to me, it was just another touchdown. You know, I expect to score every week.

Here I was, being asked a question about something that had been bothering me. I tried to keep it from getting to me, but it had been eating me for days now. Rather than be critical or negative, I tried my best to be as humble and positive about it as I could. Unfortunately, Graham wouldn't leave it alone and move on. He had to prod me with the next question.

GB: Obviously, it's not necessary, but everybody likes to be complimented, everyone likes to be congratulated for accomplishing something. And you did something that only five [other] players in the history of the NFL have done. So, how surprised were you then when the Eagles just made no public acknowledgment of it?

TO: Probably just like the statement that I said a while ago: If you align expectations with reality, you will never be disappointed. You know, their reaction shows you the type of class and integrity of an organization that they claim not to be. You know, they claim to be first class and the best organization. I just felt like it was an embarrassment. It just shows the lack of class that they had. My publicist talked to the head PR guy, and he made an excuse about [how] they didn't recognize it, or they didn't realize that it was coming up. But I know that was a blatant lie. If it would have been somebody else, they probably would have popped fireworks around the stadium.

I spoke my mind. I had no more patience. I had just been in a fight earlier that day with Hugh. No one from the organization apologized to me for the Team Ambassador's misconduct toward me. That was wrong. It was also wrong of them not to acknowledge my hundredth career touchdown reception, which was something no Philadelphia Eagle player had ever accomplished before. Only five other players in the history of the NFL ever did that. I felt I deserved ten seconds of appreciation from the fans, who would have enjoyed sharing the moment with me and my teammates.

I bit my tongue as long as I could, but after feeling underappreciated for scoring my one hundredth touchdown, and after everything that had gone on that day, I just couldn't bottle my emotions any longer. The truth came out. The organization showed a lack of class in not announcing my milestone. I thought if any other player had accomplished something of that caliber, they would have made the moment special. I resented the insult, and it festered inside me until I just had to vent. I was short of patience, as it had been a tough day, and it didn't take much to prod it out of me; I kept it in check the first time he asked, but I couldn't do so the second. The moment I spoke those words, even though it was honest speech in a free society, my career as a Philadelphia Eagle was finished.

Graham's next question and my answer put the final nails into the coffin.

> **GB:** Your friend Michael Irvin recently said that if Brett Favre was the starting quarterback for the Philadelphia Eagles, they'd be undefeated right now. What do you think of that comment?
> **TO:** I mean, that's a good assessment, I would agree with that.
> **GB:** How so?
> **TO:** I just feel like just what he brings to the table . . . I mean he's the guy. Obviously, a number of commentators will say he's a warrior. He has played with injuries. I just feel like [with] him being knowledgeable about the quarterback position, I just feel like we'd be in a better situation.

There are a couple of points here. First, Michael Irvin is in fact my friend. Michael made a strong statement that he took some heat for. I've made some strong statements as well that I took some heat for, and when he honestly agreed with what I had to say he publicly backed me. I honestly agreed, as would many experts if they were off the record, with what Michael had to say.

Second, Brett Favre is well known for being able to play well despite playing hurt. And third, Brett is perhaps the greatest quarterback ever to play the game. He won a Super Bowl and was the best in the game in his prime. He is a first-ballot Hall of Fame quarterback. How is it an insult to compliment Brett Favre?

And fourth, I never criticized Donovan. I did not say anything negative about Donovan.

Continuing with the interview, Graham asked:

> **GB:** Has the Eagles' reluctance to renegotiate your contract [made] you less willing to play hurt?

TO: No, not at all. But at the same time, I still have to be smart. Even if it wasn't a contractual situation, I still have to be smart about my body. I mean, that was the same approach that I took when I got hurt prior to playing in the playoffs or in the Super Bowl. So my approach is still the same.

It's clear to me now that Graham wanted me to say that I was less willing to play hurt because the Eagles didn't reward my efforts of the previous year with a renegotiated contract. I didn't feel that way, though. I love playing; it's my vindication, my way to fight back against my critics. I wasn't trying to hold the Eagles hostage in any way; I was determined to do everything I could to get us back to the Super Bowl.

GB: When do you plan to revisit the contract?
TO: It will be an issue after the season. I'm just going to play the season out. I'm going to go out there and let my play do the talking for me. I'm done with the contract situation until we have no more games to play.

I admit that if you wanted to cherry-pick and take things out of context, I could be portrayed as trying to cause aggravation to the organization by answering these questions. However, taking a look at the whole picture instead of the edited one, it's clear that the contract issue was behind me and I was focused on doing my job. If I had still been trying to force the team to give me a new contract, I would have mentioned the situation here and repeatedly elsewhere, but I didn't do that. I put it behind me and didn't want any problems with the Eagles.

GB: How does this all play out for you?
TO: Like I tell everybody since I've been here, I'm just here. That's just my attitude, I'm just here. I think I'm doing all the

necessary things that I'm supposed to do. I'm being professional, I'm going out there and I practice hard, I'm at my meetings. That's it; you should go out there and play.

GB: Do you feel, though, it's almost gotten to the point of no return?

TO: Point of no return as far as what?

GB: In the sense that everyone knows where you are, your stance, everyone knows where the Eagles are, their stance, and no one's going to budge.

TO: Somebody's going to have to budge sooner or later.

GB: Not you, though?

TO: Somebody got to win. Somebody got to lose.

I don't see anything wrong with what I said. I could have said I wanted to be somewhere else next year. I could have said that I was gone and unhappy. Instead, I said I'm doing my job and working hard to be professional. He kept on pushing me, backing me into a corner, and I still never said anything offensive. It was no secret that the Eagles were probably going to cut me after the season, but I didn't go there.

GB: Should Eagles fans be concerned you're putting your house up for sale?

TO: That's my prerogative if I want to sell my house or not. Maybe there is a reason why I'm putting it up for sale. My thing is I'm really not looking to be here, probably no more than the next three to five years, so who knows. I just want to be happy. If it's here then I would love to be here. If not, then you've got to move on. I have enjoyed [playing here], and I'm still enjoying football. If there is a situation where they have a change of heart and they want to come to their senses and do the right thing, I would be more than happy to be here. But, at this time, I'm being honest with myself and really trying to look toward the future. And I just don't see myself really being here. And that's not because I don't want to be here, but I just don't foresee them trying to do the necessary things to keep me here.

GB: Then what do you see happening beyond this year?

TO: I'm not sure. That's something not a lot of people are waiting to see. But I'm really just focused right now on just trying to make it to the playoffs and get the team back to the Super Bowl. So, who's to say? We may get to the playoffs, win a Super Bowl, and they might be like, "Hey! Let's pay him!" Then again, they may get to the playoffs, win or lose, get to the Super Bowl and we may have to part ways. Either way, I'm fine with it, because I'm confident in whatever I do, I'm going to be successful. It doesn't matter what anyone says about me or what anybody thinks about me; when I get on the football field, the best relationship I need is with that football. And once I get it in my hands, I make plays.

When I got sent home during training camp, I said that I didn't have to play for the Eagles and I didn't see how things could work out. I said things that were not positive toward the organization. I said things that could have alienated the fans. I had said just before this question that I love the Philly fans. I put my house up for sale because I knew the team was going to cut me. I still had some hope that if we could win the Super Bowl, maybe things could work out. Nevertheless, I wanted to be prepared for the most likely outcome—getting released after the 2005 season. The bottom line was, I was talking about winning the Super Bowl; I wasn't saying the kinds of things I was saying before I got sent home during training camp.

So much for this being a soft, positive interview. Had I told my publicist, Kim, about this, she would have shut the interview down after thirty seconds and kicked them out of the house with the heel of her boot. I thought I'd be okay because Graham was my friend and wouldn't do anything controversial that would hurt my career. I was very disappointed that Graham asked me all the questions that Kim would have told me not to answer.

After a little while, the thing I realized is that none of this was Graham's fault. I'm not mad at him; he asked the questions a good journalist would ask. I'm a grown man and I'm responsible for what I say. This was completely my fault. The blame falls on my shoulders. I've accepted the consequences and I've learned from it. I now understand that in the NFL, there is more than one game. There's the game on the field with the players, the game in the locker room with the coaches, the game in the front office with my contract, and the game everywhere, at all times, with the media lurking 24/7 to try to create a controversy. I now know about all these games, and from now on I won't engage my opponent unless I'm properly prepared. I'll be ready the next time around.

Unfortunately, I wasn't ready for the aftermath of that interview. I'd had a miserable day, and I was looking forward to it being over. I had no clue about what was going to happen next.

16

The Perfect Storm

I T seemed like the minute Graham walked out of my house, ESPN had the interview all over the TV. It was everywhere that once again I'd criticized Donovan and was trying to cause problems for the Eagles. I couldn't believe it. ESPN, just as I said in the interview, showed clips from here and there as if I had spent the whole time bashing my team. They showed about four minutes of clips out of the fifty-seven-minute interview. None of the positive things I said were anywhere to be found.

It looked as if I had set the interview up just so I could take a shot at the club. The only thing I was trying to do was help out a friend. I meant everything I said, but I wasn't looking to cause trouble. I did the best I could to honestly answer the questions in a positive way. I started off that way, but when pressed, I said what I felt about the Eagles' not acknowledging my hundredth touchdown catch. I spoke the truth and I said positive things, too, but nobody cared about that. All they cared about was that I complimented Brett Favre instead of Donovan. I guess I can't compliment another player.

I admit I shouldn't have said that about the Eagles or even answered the question on Irvin's comments about Donovan, but I did my best under the circumstances to be as positive as I was capable of being on that particular day.

Regardless of my good intentions, the Eagles acted as if I'd intentionally offended Donovan and the organization. The media came down hard on me, which put the organization and Donovan in a bad position. For that I was sorry. I didn't mean to cause a firestorm of criticism from the media. I had no idea that what I said would be newsworthy or problematic; I was shocked and I didn't understand why my comments caused such drama.

Shortly after I arrived at the Eagles' facility Friday morning, Coach Reid called my agent, Drew. He told Drew that I had to read an apology on TV in front of the media and apologize to the team for the comments that I made. Coach Reid warned Drew that if I refused to apologize to the organization, he wouldn't play me this weekend against the Redskins. His exact words to Drew were, "I will sit him this weekend."

Drew and Jason Rosenhaus made it clear to me that it was in my best interest to make the apology. I knew they were right, and I agreed to release a statement to the media. I didn't want to go on TV and apologize right after I made those remarks, because it would be embarrassing to me. Drew phoned Coach Reid and asked if I could just issue a statement on paper that he'd submit to the media on my behalf. Coach Reid refused and insisted that I read the statement on TV in front of the whole world.

I knew what I said about the team being classless was not a positive thing to say. I thought I said enough good things about wanting to win the Super Bowl and putting off my contract problem until afterward that it would even things out. I thought wrong. All Coach Reid knew was that the sports world was saying I called the Eagles classless. What I said embarrassed Coach Reid and the organization, and that wasn't what I meant to do. I was understandably in a bad mood, and when pressed, the words came out of me. I said them, and I meant what I said, but I wasn't trying to insult the club. I shouldn't have said what I did, so I agreed to do what Coach Reid wanted.

Drew and my publicist, Kim, drafted an apology for me to read. Coach Reid rushed me to read it. Drew and Kim emailed to the Eagles what they drafted for my apology.

Here is what I read in front of the cameras:

> I've had an opportunity to talk with the Eagles organization and I have learned that the team does not recognize individual achievements. It has been brought to my attention that I have offended the organization and my teammates. Therefore, I would like to apologize for any derogatory comments toward them.

What nobody but Kim, Drew, and Jason knew was that I'd crossed out the part of the draft that apologized to Donovan. The reason I didn't apologize to Donovan was that I didn't think I owed him an apology for what I said. Yes, I insulted the team by calling the organization classless. But regarding Donovan, I only agreed with Michael Irvin by complimenting one of the greatest quarterbacks to ever play the game. Most NFL coaches and scouts would agree privately with what I said—though after seeing the media's reaction to me, they'd be too scared or too politically correct to admit it publicly. I did apologize to my "teammates," which includes Donovan.

The players, except for Donovan, didn't think my comments were that big a deal. One teammate, defensive end Sam Rayburn, shrugged off the remarks to the media, saying, "It's just TO being TO. It's just him talking."

ESPN showed the apology over and over again. It was embarrassing. They wrote on ESPN.com, "It's unlikely that [Owens] would be suspended now that [he] apologized."

I thought it was over and that I could get back to practicing for the upcoming game against the Redskins. However, Coach Reid did not see it that way. He called Drew and said the apology on national TV to the organization and my teammates wasn't good enough. He told Drew that I would have to apologize to Donovan in front of the whole team.

I couldn't believe it. I had just embarrassed myself in front of the whole sports world and apologized for what I said. Now I had to go make a special apology to Donovan in front of the whole team? No, not like that. I didn't have a problem apologizing to Donovan, because what I said apparently had an unintentional, negative effect on him, but I was going to talk to him by myself.

I didn't think I should have to go before the whole team and apologize once more. I'm a principled person and I wouldn't do that!

When I told Drew this, he called Coach Reid and tried extremely hard to persuade him that I would talk to Donovan, but not in front of the whole team.

Coach Reid refused and told Drew that if I didn't apologize to Donovan ASAP, "I'll be forced to sit him for a game."

When Drew told me this, he tried to persuade me to compromise and do what was necessary to play, but I told him that I wouldn't do it. Drew knew me well enough to realize that nothing he could say or do would make me change my mind, but he still tried.

After practice, I went home and called in for my weekly radio show. I went on the show and said before the nation that I was only agreeing with Michael Irvin's opinion. I said that the interview was taken out of context. My exact words were, "This is one I really regret . . . I said earlier in the interview that we would have a better record if Donovan wasn't injured."

I thought that I made things right with those comments. It

wasn't an apology, but it was an explanation that defended Donovan.

The next morning, Donovan called a team meeting. He said that players who did not do things a certain way around there have come and gone. In front of the team, he declared that everyone in the room was either with him or against him. He challenged anyone against him to speak up. No one did. I wasn't against him, and I didn't want to start a confrontation in front of everyone.

I walked out of there prepared to talk to him when things settled down.

Next thing I know, I'm sitting in Coach Reid's office. I hoped that Coach Reid would take some responsibility for what Hugh said and did, and that he would understand that I made those remarks in the interview just a few hours after the fight. I hoped Coach Reid would look at the positive things I said in the interview. I hoped . . . but it didn't happen that way. Instead, he gave me an ultimatum: Apologize to Donovan or "sit" the Redskin game. My instant response was "sit"; I thought I would be declared inactive for that one game.

I knew at the time that I would pay a big price for taking a stand. I never dreamed how big it would be. Coach Reid never said he would suspend me, or that he'd sit me beyond that one game against the Redskins. I could see in his eyes that he was disappointed, but I could also see that he hated to do it as much as I did.

We both had our pride and principles. The problem was they conflicted. I respected Coach Reid for doing what he had to do. I didn't agree with it, but I knew it was hard for him to do. What I did not respect was being ordered to do something that went against my principles. It wasn't just pride; I objected to being forced to apologize in the manner I was being ordered to do it. I was being bullied all over again. I could not allow that to happen.

It was killing me that I was going to miss the Redskins game. Playing on Sundays was my salvation. It would have been so much easier to give in and compromise. It was brutal not to play. However, I couldn't have lived with myself if I sold out my self-respect and dignity because the Eagles forced me to do so. Every man has to look at himself in the mirror.

When I got home Saturday, Coach Reid sent me the following fax: "We are suspending you for conduct detrimental to the team, for this week's game against the Washington Redskins."

I knew it was time to take my medicine. It was only one game, but Sundays are my chance to win and celebrate, and I was going to have to get through the weekend without that.

To make things worse, news broke of the fight between Hugh and me. I knew everybody would assume that I'd started it by saying something; nobody would think that I was defending myself and responding to Hugh's attack both verbally and physically. The media blew it up as if I had done something wrong. No one was going to let the facts get in the way of their story. No one was going to let the truth stop them from criticizing me.

When the game came on, I turned the TV off. I didn't want to watch; it was too painful not to be out there with my teammates.

The Eagles lost a close game to the Redskins, 17–10. The offense got the ball down to the Washington seven yard line, second and four, in the final two minutes and couldn't get it across. I know in my heart that I would have made the difference; if I didn't score myself, by drawing double or even triple coverage I would have made it much easier for one of my teammates to get open.

Unfortunately for me, Coach Reid, my teammates, and the Philly fans, Donovan did not see it that way. Donovan had the following comments after the game:

> Obviously it is tough losing a guy of his caliber, his ability, but *I think we might be better off* [emphasis added]. I think what we did tonight, we showed that we played well together. I think we also showed that when given the opportunity, guys can make plays for us. We're 4–4. We're not 1–7. I think that is the way to look at it. For the guys in the locker room, we win together and we lose together . . . It was unfortunate that we didn't win this game, but I think it may be a stepping-stone for us to move forward.

So let me get this straight: The offense gets ten points, has three shots from the Redskin seven yard line and fails to make the play. The defense put the offense in position to win and the offense didn't get it done. Yet somehow Donovan concludes that they played well, made plays, and were better off without me?

I wasn't happy the team lost without me or about what Donovan had to say. I told myself just to get through the day, that everything would be back to normal tomorrow. But tomorrow never came.

With his statement that the Eagles "might be better off" without me, Donovan made it clear that it was either him or me. With my bonus coming up next year, at my age, it was certainly not going to be me.

Coach Reid called a press conference Monday morning, November 7, and announced that I would be suspended four games without pay, including the Redskins game, and placed on the inactive list with pay for the remaining regular-season and playoff games.

Coach Reid said that I was suspended because of a "large

number of situations that accumulated over a period of time" and that I "had been warned repeatedly about the consequences of [my] actions."

According to him, "We gave Terrell every opportunity to avoid this outcome. . . . The league has been notified by the players' union that they will be grieving our right to take that action. Therefore, there is nothing more that I can say at this point."

What Coach Reid said wasn't exactly true or fair. Yes, it was true that I was warned I would be sent home and I had the opportunity to avoid that. However, it wasn't true that I was ever warned that I'd be suspended for more than the Redskins game. If Coach Reid had told me or given me or Drew any indication whatsoever that he was going to suspend me and send me home for the rest of the games, I would have found a way to make things work. I would have asked Coach Reid to let me handle things my way and give me some time to work things out with Donovan. I never dreamed that I was going to be suspended for the remainder of the season. I never knew that those would be the consequences. I was never given any indication that was a remote possibility. I didn't think the Eagles would kill their season like that.

I was stunned when I got the news. Coach Reid didn't talk to me before making the decision. They suspended me for the season and made the announcement to the public before talking to me and giving me a chance to work things out.

I wanted that chance. I did a lot of soul searching that weekend. I spoke with my pastor about everything. He explained to me that although I didn't mean to criticize Donovan, my words had that effect. I made a statement that unintentionally caused my teammate embarrassment. Regardless of what Donovan did to me, regardless of how I felt about Donovan, his actions were irrelevant. The only thing that mattered was my actions, and I had to be accountable for them. He explained to me that when a man does something that is hurtful to someone else, even if it is accidental, that man has to make amends.

Having had the time to cool off from the craziness of the fight, the media, the ultimatum, the embarrassment, and the bullying, I agreed with him.

I didn't change my mind because I'd been suspended for the season; I changed my mind because I thought it was the right thing to do. Having suffered through the weekend, I had the chance to step out of my shoes and look at things from a different perspective.

I had gone through an absolutely crazy, mind-boggling couple of days, a perfect storm of insult, anger, hurt, and re-criminations. What were the odds of all those things happening all at once? Think about it.

I woke up Thursday morning trying to rehabilitate my reinjured ankle. I was trying to get ready to play on it against the Redskins and risk my career all over again. That right there is enough to stress anyone out.

Then the Team Ambassador came deliberately looking for me, and in front of the team, he yelled profanities about me and accused me of faking the injury. To go through what I went through and then be accused of being the type of player who would fake an injury to avoid playing the game I love—that was the lowest insult anyone ever offered me.

I stood up to him like a man and asked him what he wanted to do. He responded by throwing the first punch and tried to take me out.

Then I went home and did an interview to help a young friend out, and he came on as if it were *60 Minutes*. I tried to be positive with my initial answers, but after the events of the day I was too emotional to be calm and cool; I lost my con-trol and said things I wouldn't have said publicly otherwise. ESPN aired the interview in the most negative light possible, editing out all the good things I had to say about the Eagles and Donovan. The media took my comments and blew them up into a huge controversy—exactly what I had worked so hard to avoid since late August.

Coach Reid called me in not to ask what happened with Hugh or to apologize for him, but to demand that I apologize to the team. Releasing a written apology to the media wasn't good enough; I had to read it in front of the media in an embarrassing manner. So I apologized to the Eagles and to my teammates. Yet Coach Reid did not accept that, either.

He gave me an ultimatum. I needed a little bit of time to cool off, but no, they weren't going to give me the slightest break here. I had to apologize the way they wanted, when they wanted. After everything that had happened to me, after being insulted, humiliated, and attacked far worse than anyone else, I was too emotional to apologize. I could only see my point of view and no one else's. So I got sent home and had all that time to think things over. By game time Sunday morning, I was remorseful and looking forward to going to work Monday morning and making things right with Donovan. It really hurt, but it also settled me down to miss that game. Then Donovan added salt to the wound by coming out and saying the Eagles would be better off with me gone. Donovan's statement created a public ultimatum for Coach Reid. Left with no choice, Coach Reid suspended me for the season. If that wasn't a "Perfect Storm" that hit me, then I don't know what would be.

My first reaction was that they couldn't suspend me or anyone else for the rest of the season; the league rules say that a team can only discipline a player for four games. The Buccaneers in 2003 sent Keyshawn Johnson home for the final six games, but Keyshawn decided to accept being sent home as long as he got paid. He was content to take the money. I wasn't. No amount of money would shut down my desire to play.

I spoke with my agents and the NFLPA. They told me the Eagles did not have the authority to discipline me for more than four games. The Eagles wanted to send me home for eight games. The NFLPA said the Eagles had violated the Collective Bargaining Agreement and ignored my rights. They responded by immediately filing a grievance on my behalf to challenge the suspension.

However, first things first. I thought it was necessary for me to make a statement. The Eagles had wronged me. I could not believe that this really was happening to me. I was angry and hurt. The haters out there were loving every minute of it. My family was upset. This was very hard for me to accept.

I thought it was horrible that they were depriving me of my livelihood. They were going to suspend me for four games, fine me about eight hundred thousand dollars, and sit me the remaining four games. Missing the Redskins game was tough enough, but having to miss the rest of the season was unbearable. They really stuck it to me. It didn't have to be that way, but that was what they wanted to do.

I could have responded by lashing out at the Eagles and stating how unfair their punishment was. I could have been extremely negative and created an even bigger controversy.

Instead I chose to hold a press conference the next day, on Tuesday, November 8, where I read the following statement:

As you know, I have been suspended and told that I cannot play football the rest of the season. I am a football player, that is what I do. It really hurts me not to be part of the team anymore. I came here to take the Eagles to the Super Bowl and win the big game. When I got hurt last year, everyone said that my season was over. I fought hard to prove the world wrong and do everything possible, including risking my career, to help the Eagles win the Super Bowl. And I think that mentality I have, my greatest strength, can sometimes be my greatest weakness. I am a fighter, I always have been and I always will be. I fight for what I think is right.

In doing so, I alienated a lot of my fans and teammates. To those fans who supported me through these tough times, I thank you for that support. To every single Philadelphia fan out there, I want you to know that I am sorry things worked out this way. To you, I apologize.

To my teammates, a lot of you have been a friend to me and I appreciate that. I can't tell you how much I wanted to fight along your side to take this team to victory. It was very painful for me to not be with you against the Redskins last weekend and it is even more painful for me to not be with you this weekend.

I would like to reiterate my respect for Donovan McNabb as a quarterback and as a teammate. I apologize to him for any comments that may have been negative.

To my head coach, Andy Reid, I owe you an apology. You and I were in a tough spot this year. I know you were just trying to coach this team and we did not see eye to eye sometimes, but on the practice field and on game day, you knew you could count on me to give you my best. We had a lot of wins together and I thank you for that. I respect you as a coach and as a person.

To Joe Banner and to [owner Jeffrey] Lurie, I understand that all along you were doing what you believed to be in the best interest of the Philadelphia Eagles. I apologize to the both of you as well.

In conclusion, as I said before, this is very painful for me to be in this position. It really hurts me not to be part of the team anymore. I came here to help the Eagles get to the Super Bowl and win the big game by not only being a dominant player but also a team player. I can bring that.

After I read the apology, the media started shouting questions and insults at the same time. Drew stepped forward and defended me. The media were reporting that Drew was going to walk away from me, and we wanted to clear that up. Drew stated that the media were treating me unfairly. They responded with one negative question after another. To which Drew replied, "Next question."

The apology was sincere and, as I expected, it made no difference to the Eagles. They responded by immediately releasing a statement that their position remained the same. I knew that my statement wasn't going to make a difference to them, but it did to me.

Those were the last public remarks I made during 2005. I think they represented me well. Of course, no one cared about the integrity or the sincerity of what I had to say. Instead, everyone looked to the upcoming showdown.

The date for my grievance hearing was set for November 18—just ten days later. The arbitrator to decide the case was Richard Bloch. The NFLPA told Drew, Jason, and me that his previous decisions were very consistent with labor law principles, NFL case precedent, and the NFL Collective Bargaining Agreement. They viewed his presence as a big positive for the case. I thought I was finally going to get a fair shake and looked forward to having my day in court.

The next day, Coach Reid sent me a letter that detailed the team's basis for my unprecedented nine-game suspension. They put together a laundry list of my supposed misconduct. Ironically, Sal Paolantonio discussed the details of the letter on TV before I even received it. I learned of their reasons through him.

The reasons the Eagles cited for disciplining me more severely than any player in the recent history of the NFL were the following:

1. The ESPN.com interview with Graham Bensinger.
2. Failure to apologize to the satisfaction of Coach Reid.
3. Being late to a mandatory offensive team meeting.
4. Failure to comply with the team rules regarding travel attire on every road trip despite numerous reminders from Coach Reid in team meetings.
5. Parking in reserved handicapped and coaches' spots that I was not permitted to park in.
6. Being involved in a fight with an employee in the training room.

These six reasons are why I was suspended for the year and fined eight hundred thousand dollars, my salary for four games. Compared to what other players have done in the NFL and other sports, the list is a joke. I didn't break the law. I exercised my freedom of speech. And I got hit the hardest? What they did to me was wrong. I couldn't wait to get a fair and impartial hearing so I could get some justice.

It was a long week. Radio and TV shows were desperately trying to persuade me to go on the air, but I understandably wanted to keep things quiet until the hearing. One show responded by saying I was greedy and bad for the sport.

What hypocrites! Here they were begging and offering to pay me to do the show so they could boost their own ratings, and they were calling me greedy! The media never cease to amaze me.

The media had a field day the night before our next game, at home against Dallas. One radio station held a funeral for me and threw their 81 jerseys in a casket. One of the talk-show hosts actually burned an 81 jersey and threw the ashes in the end zone.

The game itself wound up being the kiss of death for the Eagles' season. That wasn't how it started, however; the first half went well, with Donovan scoring on a two-yard scramble.

In the fourth quarter, the Eagles had the game won, leading 20–14 with 2:43 left in the game. They had the ball at midfield and were in position to take command, drain the clock, and put the game out of reach with a field goal.

They'd had success all night running the ball and throwing short passes to the running back and tight end. However, Donovan was not successful throwing to his wide receivers; the two starting wideouts combined for six catches and fifty-seven yards. I alone was averaging seven catches a game for over one hundred yards.

With the game all but over, Donovan "made one of the costliest mistakes of his seven-year career," according to ESPN.com. Rather than continue to dink and dunk the ball off to the running back or tight end, Donovan tried to throw the ball downfield. ESPN described the play as follows:

> McNabb's poorly thrown pass was picked off by [Roy] Williams, who outran McNabb as the quarterback tried to tackle him. . . . Donovan McNabb went to his knees and buried his face in the grass. The pain from his groin injury and his game-turning interception were far worse than anything Terrell Owens could've done. The Eagles' problems are much bigger than T.O. now.

The game was lost to a late fourth-quarter interception return. The Eagles were now 4–5; they'd lost three in a row and were in trouble.

After the game, Donovan told the media, "I'm tired of answering TO questions. TO is not here."

I wasn't there, but I wanted to be. And, as it turned out, the player who got seriously wounded for the season that night was Donovan. He tore his groin trying to make the tackle on the interception return for a touchdown, and his season was over.

That meant backup quarterback Mike McMahon was now in charge of the season. Too bad he wasn't in charge of the team. He and I were friends and got along well. He wanted me back in the worst way, but the only way I was going to get back on the team was by winning the case that Friday.

Leading up to the arbitration hearing, I wanted to know what kind of case I had, and I discussed everything with my legal team. The boss was Richard Berthelsen, the general counsel of the NFLPA. He hired the law firm of Dewey Ballantine to represent me. The firm had four attorneys handling my case—Jeffrey Kessler, David Feher, Adam Kaiser, and David Greenspan.

Now, I haven't watched a lot of the courtroom drama shows on TV, but if there's a more impressive group of attorneys out there than these five guys, then they must have their own series. Along with Drew, Jason, and Kim, I sat down with them the night before the hearing and we all went over the details of my case.

They explained to me that our argument consisted of the following six legal points.

First, the nine-game suspension exceeded the maximum discipline permitted under the Collective Bargaining Agreement (CBA), which provides that, for conduct detrimental, a club may impose a "maximum fine of an amount equal to one week's salary and/or suspension without pay for a period not to exceed four (4) weeks." It doesn't take a great legal mind to realize that a nine-game suspension is greater than a four-game suspension, and therefore the suspension exceeds the maximum discipline allowed by the CBA.

Second, the nine-game suspension violated basic principles of industrial double jeopardy. No, that's not a category for Alex Trebek's show. Double jeopardy, they told me, is a situation in which a person is punished two separate times for the same offense. In my case, the Eagles first suspended me on November 5, for one game. The suspension was imposed after the November 3 ESPN.com interview and what they considered the unsatisfactory November 4 apology. Then, on November 7, the Eagles hit me with a second wave of discipline for the same conduct and increased my suspension to eight more regular-season games. This second round of discipline, without any new misconduct on my behalf, was a violation of basic federal labor law, according to my attorneys.

Third, the CBA and federal labor law require that everyone be treated the same. That appealed to me because I was tired of the NFL having two sets of rules—one for me and one for everyone else. The NFLPA negotiated the CBA with NFL management to provide that team discipline must be uniform for everyone. This way, there wouldn't be any double standards. The NFLPA wanted to make sure that all players had protection from clubs wanting to discipline one player more harshly than another for similar offenses. My attorneys also said that federal labor law doesn't allow employers to impose disproportionate discipline. They showed me that players on the Eagles, other NFL players, and players from other professional sports had done things similar to, or far more serious than, any conduct of mine even alleged by the Eagles, but they got far less punishment. Comparing my actions to the actions of those other guys, my attorneys felt that the Eagles had no legal basis to support the one-game suspension, let alone a nine-game suspension, for my exercise of speech. They pointed out that there was no loyalty clause in my contract that prohibited me from making certain comments.

Fourth, the Eagles were supposed to discipline me in a progressive manner—that is, to go from a small fine to a larger one to a one-game suspension and then to a two-game suspension, and so on. They went from fining me $150 for being late to a meeting to a nine-game suspension with an eight-hundred-thousand-dollar fine. That is not exactly progressive.

Fifth, my comments were made in an interview that took place just a few hours after Hugh made his infuriating accusations and tried to punch my face in. For all I knew, management had sent him in there, and they never apologized to me for his misconduct, so it was understandable that I would be upset with the organization.

And sixth, as an employee, I was entitled to due process. That means the Eagles were required to do some type of investigation into the facts before suspending me for the season. They never even asked me about the fight with Hugh, but listed the fight as one of the reasons I was suspended. They completely disregarded my right to due process.

For all these reasons, we felt that our case was a lock. Every expert I saw on TV and the Internet agreed, predicting that arbitrator Richard Bloch would reduce the suspension to one or two games instead of nine. We even thought we had an excellent chance of getting back pay for a good part of the two games I would miss before the decision would come out.

With everyone thinking that I was going to be reinstated, it seemed like a waste of time to go through with the hearing. I wanted to come back and get the team back on the right track. Although the Eagles' record was 4–5, the season was still there for the taking. I knew I could come in and put the team back on the winning track, even without Donovan.

I wasn't the only one thinking that. A lot of my teammates at this point wanted me back. I had made a very sincere apology and I think that won back most of the guys who were against me. Jeremiah Trotter thought so, too. He called me while I was in the hotel suite meeting with my attorneys. He told me that he had talked to Coach Reid and that all I had to do was call Coach Reid and let him know I was sorry and would make things right with Donovan. Jeremiah was so insistent and eager to have me back that he came over to the hotel and met with me.

Jeremiah fought for me. This was the toughest guy on the team, the undisputed team leader. Every person on that team likes, admires, and respects Jeremiah, with good reason.

He told the media, "We would love to have TO back, we would love to have him back because we love what he brings to the team. It would definitely make us a better team." He even added that "Andy loves TO. But, you know, as a head coach, you've got so many things to worry about the last thing you want to worry about is outside distractions other than coaching the football team."

After Jeremiah came over and talked with me, I called Coach Reid. He didn't answer, so I left a message. During my drive home, he called me back.

He spoke to me not only as a coach but as a friend. We talked for a long time. He complimented me for taking the step to call him and apologize for my actions. I took responsibility for what happened and he respected that. He wanted to know if I could make things right with Donovan. I told him that I definitely would. I let him know that I had actually called Donovan last week to try to straighten things out, but that Donovan hadn't called me back. I told him the reasons why I was angry with Donovan, and he gave me some advice that I will never forget.

Coach Reid said that I should learn to focus on the positives of people, instead of the negatives. He was right. I never let go of Donovan's negatives, and I focused on them, disregarding the fact that he has a very fun, likable personality and wants to win. I thanked him for that advice and told him that I would do that.

Then I said that the hearing tomorrow was unnecessary. I

told him he should bring me back, I would work things out with Donovan and help the team win that Sunday against the Giants. I really tried to sell him on it. Coach Reid responded by laughing and telling me in a joking, manly way that he loved me. It bothered me right then and there that we were all in this terrible position. I could tell that he was conflicted and wanted me back. He ended the conversation by telling me to stay by the phone and he would call me back.

I knew it could go either way with Coach Reid. Even though it looked as if my case was in the bag, I remembered something Jason said in front of all the attorneys. He told me that anything could happen, and it would be the right move to work something out with Coach Reid. That was in the back of my mind as I talked with Coach Reid and then waited around for his call.

He called back about an hour later. I don't know who he spoke to, but somebody killed it. He was unhappy and almost apologetic, saying that we should see what happened in the arbitration. I couldn't believe it. Somebody told him not to take me back.

I called some of my teammates, and they couldn't believe it, especially Jeremiah. They were very upset about it. I just wanted to come back and play. I didn't care if Donovan was there or not. I wanted to play with Donovan. I wanted to play with Mike, too. I made up my mind at the start of the season to do my best to have a great season and that was what I wanted to do. I wasn't trying to take the team away from Donovan, but I guess it seemed that way to some. I didn't want to believe something so harsh, but it was the only explanation that made sense to me.

Coach Reid wouldn't have told Jeremiah to ask me to call him, he wouldn't have talked to me the way he did, he wouldn't have opened the door, if management was opposed to it. I had been suspended and missed two games already, a pretty stiff punishment. They'd proved their point. I would have thought this was a decision for the head coach, not the front office, anyway. Besides, anyone who knows how things are run around there knows that Andy makes the football decisions; if Coach Reid didn't have the power to take me back, why would he tell Jeremiah that he would take me back if I called him and said the right things to him? If it wasn't the front office, and the overwhelming majority of the players wanted me back, who else could Coach Reid have talked to? It apparently came down to a choice between me and Donovan, and since I was only likely to be there for seven more games and Donovan was the team's quarterback for years to come, Coach Reid didn't have much of a choice.

I was disappointed that we had to do things the hard way. I was so close to coming back to the team. I thought the fans and my teammates deserved that. So close . . . but I guess that only counts for horseshoes and hand grenades.

17
The Hearing

I **WOKE** up disappointed that I had to go through with the hearing, but I at least looked forward to watching Richard Berthelsen and Jeffrey Kessler go to work on the Eagles' attorneys. Those two were some bad dudes to mess with in the legal world. Jeff is never going to be mistaken for a professional athlete, but this guy is without a doubt a total monster. He has the tenacity of a real competitor and more brain power than anybody I ever met. He has a look like he can verbally abuse someone to death. I was very glad he was on my side and would never want him cross-examining me.

Although Jeff was the man at his firm, the boss was NFLPA general counsel Richard Berthelsen. Although Richard would concede that Jeff Kessler just might be the smartest person on the planet, he seemed just as smart and tough. Richard is tall, imposing, and talks to you in a very authoritative manner. Although he seems like a good guy, I felt as if I were back in school and sitting down talking to the principal in his office when he talked to me, and that was when he was being nice to me. It was obvious to me that Richard knew his job and was well prepared. Richard has a natural sense of confidence about himself and it rubbed off on me. Being around him, I felt very empowered by our case. I could see why he's a leader within the NFLPA. Richard was like the coach calling the plays, and Jeff went out and executed them.

Jeff's partner was David Feher. David is very different from Jeff. David is no doubt Mr. IQ as well, but he's very poised and strategic in the way he talks. It seemed to me that while Jeff attacks like a brawler, David probes for weakness like a boxer with a great jab. If Sherlock Holmes were an attorney instead of a private detective, he would have been exactly like David. The three of them made an excellent team.

Working with Jeff and David were two younger guys, Adam Kaiser and David Greenspan. Adam had an excellent understanding of the law and broke things down for me so I could follow them. He worked extremely hard putting together the nuts and bolts of the case. I could see he did the research and was responsible for the details of their strategy. I liked Adam; he knew football and was extremely knowledgeable about the background of the Eagles. David Greenspan was a cool guy. He was sharp and a pretty smooth operator.

With these guys and the rest of our team in my corner, I knew I couldn't lose. After talking the whole day before and into the evening, I was ready that morning when I drove up to the arbitration meeting place at a hotel in Philly with Drew, Kim, and Jason.

We all took our seats in the meeting room. Since this was such a high-profile case, there were a lot of people in the room.

On one side of the table sat the NFL attorneys. Behind them in separate chairs sat Eagles president Joe Banner, his director of football administration, Howie Roseman, and several more attorneys.

On the other side of the table sat Jeff Kessler, Richard Berthelsen, David Feher, and their colleagues Adam Kaiser and David Greenspan. I sat behind them against the wall with Drew, Kim, and Jason.

Richard Bloch and the stenographer sat at the head of the table between the NFL attorney and Jeff Kessler.

The Eagles presented their opening statement first. The day before, both sides had submitted a prehearing brief to the arbitrator and to each other, stating their positions. Having read our arguments, they opened up by stating their case that I'd committed numerous infractions to intentionally sabotage the team as part of a grand scheme to force the Eagles to renegotiate my contract. He went through how I caused problems and did all these terrible things. While he was speaking, he kept looking at me as if he could intimidate me. It didn't work.

They actually showed footage of some of my interviews. I couldn't believe it when they showed video of me being asked one question and then edited the tape to show my answer to a separate question. That was shady, real dirty.

I looked at Jeff Kessler while the other attorney was talking. He looked like a mad dog champing at the bit to get after it. When it was his turn, Jeff stood up and destroyed each of their arguments one by one and just slaughtered them. The other side looked as if they were going to puke by the time Kessler finished with his opening statement. They knew they were in for a long day against Richard and this guy.

The first witness they called was Coach Reid. At this point, Drew had to leave the room because he was a potential witness.

My lawyers explained to me how direct examinations and cross-examinations work: Typically, the longer a guy is kept on the stand, the better it's going for the examiner. If the witness is not helping the case, he gets dismissed quickly.

Although I felt extremely confident after Jeff's opening statement, when Coach Reid took a seat next to the arbitrator, I got a bad vibe. Richard Bloch looked giddy to meet Coach Reid. He lit up when Coach Reid testified. Bloch had been stoic and all business toward me when we started, but he looked at Andy as if he was his biggest fan.

The direct examination of Coach Reid by his own attorney started with what happened in training camp and why he sent me home in August. After going through all of that, he was asked to explain what happened that led to my November suspension.

Through it all, Coach Reid testified honestly and fairly. He told it pretty much like it happened. He came across as very sincere and likable.

Coach Reid could have tried to attack my character, but he didn't. It seemed he knew he was going to lose the case and have to take me back, so he didn't cross the line.

Jeff Kessler and Richard Berthelsen had no such problems. Let's get one thing straight—Coach Reid is a very smart guy and can handle himself in any crowd of Ivy Leaguers. I'm sure Coach Reid could have beaten the heck out of any other attorneys, but Berthelsen and Kessler are just in a class by themselves. They made the opposing attorneys look average, and a football guy like Coach Reid didn't stand a chance against them. With Richard counseling and directing Jeff, it was almost unfair.

Jeff kept Coach Reid on the stand for what seemed, to Coach Reid and everyone else in the room, like forever. There was one critical part of the testimony in which Jeff asked Coach Reid why he deactivated me for the remainder of the season after the four-game suspension, and Coach Reid answered "conduct detrimental."

Shortly after that, we took a break. As soon as we got into our private room, it looked as if Jeff and the guys were doing cartwheels and somersaults. They explained to me that Coach Reid had just killed the Eagles' case. By admitting he punished me for the remainder of the season for conduct detrimental, Coach Reid had declared that he punished me beyond the four-game-suspension maximum allowed. The Eagles had been arguing that they were only punishing me for four weeks, which is within the rules; they took the position that sending me home with pay after the suspension was not a violation of the four-game maximum because sending me home was not discipline. Since I was being paid, even though I was sent home and not allowed to be part of the team, the Eagles claimed I wasn't being disciplined.

In response, Jeff cited a previous case in Major League Baseball, which had actually been decided by Bloch himself. In that case, Bloch ruled that in determining whether management's actions were in fact discipline, the substance of the case mattered, not the form. Bloch established the precedent that management can't get around maximum discipline provisions by calling the substance of the punishment by another name. That set the precedent that whatever management calls it, a response by management to perceived misconduct is discipline, regardless of the form it takes. Bloch himself created the precedent that deactivation is a form of punishment.

Although this was a situation new to the NFL, many cases in baseball had previously established that deactivation with pay was in fact punishment. This was a no-brainer, and was a major reason why all the legal experts felt the Eagles were going to lose this case badly.

As Jeff's cross-examination continued, Coach Reid's testimony served up their case to us on a silver platter.

Jeff asked Andy questions about our double-jeopardy argument. Coach Reid admitted that between the Saturday he sent me home and the Monday he suspended me for the season, there was no new conduct to cause him to increase the discipline against me. Coach Reid was honest and testified that he did talk with Joe Banner over the weekend about the fact that if they extended the suspension beyond one game, I would be in breach of my contract and they could try to get back some of my signing bonus money.

Jeff pointed out that according to the Eagles' position, Coach Reid could tell me to go home and sit in a closet for the next *six years* so long as they paid me. That wouldn't be punishment, according to the Eagles. Where would it end if teams could sit a guy indefinitely for the same misconduct?

Jeff made it clear that the Eagles were disciplining me twice for the same infraction, which is double jeopardy. Coach Reid never told me or Drew he was going to "suspend" me. Coach Reid said he would sit me for one game. He never gave me any notice that I could be suspended for more than one game, let alone the rest of the season.

In fact, the first suspension letter the Eagles sent me read, "We are suspending you for conduct detrimental to the team for this week's game against the Washington Redskins. I will contact you next week regarding your status going forward." The letter does not say that the Eagles' investigation of the matter would continue, that additional suspensions or fines might follow, or that the Eagles were reserving their right to impose further discipline. The bottom line is that at first I was given notice that I would be disciplined for one game; then all of a sudden, after being punished for that game, they punished me a second time when they suspended me for the rest of the season without ever giving me any notice that they might do so. The lack of notice in the first letter and in Coach Reid's first talk with me made the second punishment a clear-cut case of double jeopardy. The team could not do that, according to the CBA and labor law.

Jeff and Richard then focused on each of the six reasons for the discipline. A key fact is that the Eagles could not legally discipline me now for anything that happened in training camp. They had already disciplined me back in August by sending me home from camp; they couldn't discipline me for the same thing again in November, because that would be double jeopardy. They also, according to the CBA, have forty-five days to discipline me for any misconduct; you can't discipline a player in November for something he did in August. The Eagles conceded this in their suspension letter by citing six things that all took place during the regular season.

The Eagles had the burden of proving with clear and convincing evidence that the six infractions leading to the nine-game suspension and eight-hundred-thousand-dollar loss of pay rose to the level of what a reasonable person would conclude was conduct detrimental to the team that would warrant such a penalty. (Okay, my coauthor helped me out with that one and maybe a couple of other parts of this chapter.)

Jeff and Richard then went to work on the six infractions. First was the interview. Coach Reid testified that when he first looked at the comments, he didn't see some of the positive things that I had said. However, when Coach Reid took a second look at the unedited transcript of what I said, he acknowledged that I said some good things as well.

Continuing with the interview, Jeff discussed my fight with Hugh Douglas and pointed out to Coach Reid how that whole incident could make any reasonable person say negative things about a team. He also pointed out that I didn't say anything derogatory about Donovan, that I was agreeing with my friend Michael Irvin about Brett Favre's greatness rather than saying anything about Donovan.

Regarding the apology, Jeff noted that I was angry over both the fight and having been embarrassed enough already with the first apology. Jeff explained that after everything I had gone through, there was no way I could immediately go before the team and prostrate myself in front of Donovan and the guys. Jeff pointed out that Drew told Coach Reid that I needed some time and that I would take care of it my way.

After being attacked, it was certainly reasonable for me to need a little time to cool off before being forced to apologize a second time.

About my being late to a mandatory meeting, I was late one time due to unusually bad traffic and was fined $150 for that incident. I admit that I am guilty as charged on this one.

Failure to wear proper attire while traveling on road trips was the fourth reason given for my extreme punishment. The Eagles made the argument that my wearing Irvin's jersey after a game was a terrible offense. Coach Reid destroyed that argument himself when he admitted that he didn't think the jersey was a big deal. He also acknowledged that he thought the tuxedo was actually amusing.

Thus far, my terrible infractions amounted to a $150 fine.

The fifth offense was parking in reserved spots at the facility. Coach Reid agreed that players who are rehabbing often park in those spots because it's hard for us to walk if we're injured. He also acknowledged that other players on the team parked in those spots, too, and were not disciplined.

And finally the fight, which was described by the media as serious misconduct and evidence that I was a troublemaker. Coach Reid admitted that I wasn't at fault for the fight, that Hugh was wrong to accuse me of faking and was wrong to start the confrontation and to throw a punch at me. He basically admitted that I was the victim and had done nothing wrong.

Okay, so let's take a quick recess here. At this point, I want to ask you to reconsider what I had done that I should be punished more severely than any NFL player in the last forty years. Of the six reasons given for the punishment, the first two incidents, I believe, were understandable, because of the way I had been insulted, humiliated, and attacked. I admit that I was guilty on the third count of being late to a meeting and deserved the $150 fine. As for the fourth count, about my clothing, Coach Reid admitted that it wasn't a big deal worth disciplining me for. Regarding the parking, that too was no big deal in his eyes. And finally, I wasn't at fault for the fight at all. Hugh himself later testified that he started it, he was at fault, he was wrong, he threw the first punch, and he regrets it (which I respected him for, by the way). Jeff didn't have to beat up Hugh because Hugh beat him to the punch.

These are the reasons Jeff and Richard kept Coach Reid on the stand for so long. Coach Reid was honest and appeared to have no problem sinking their case against me. My attorneys were thrilled with the way Coach Reid's testimony went. I have to admit, I was feeling pretty good and agreed that things were definitely going our way.

What Jeff had established through the brief and his arguments was that the Eagles had to show that my alleged misconduct was what a reasonable person would consider as conduct detrimental, and the only actions that mattered were ones that took place after I returned to training camp. All the controversial statements I made in the off-season and in the early part of training camp were irrelevant. Only the six acts of misconduct cited by the Eagles could be considered.

With the Eagles' case for those six counts in shambles, the other issue to be determined was whether the punishment fit the crime. Even if the fight had never taken place and the interview was considered to be misconduct, you still have to compare the reaction to those in other discipline cases. The all-important rule in the CBA states, "Discipline will be imposed uniformly within a Club on all players for the same offense." This means that there is only one set of rules that must be applied to everyone in the same fashion. The CBA specifically makes clear that there can't be one set of rules for me and another for everyone else.

NFL case law interpreted that rule to set the precedent that "any discipline program requires that individuals subject to that program understand, with reasonable certainty, what results will occur if they breached established rules." This means that a player must have a reasonable notion of the punishment likely to result from misconduct.

The way I get this understanding is by the team warning me, or by the discipline given to other players who committed similar offenses. The CBA demands that the Eagles treat me the same way everyone else is treated. Therefore, we looked at other disciplinary cases, with the Eagles and elsewhere.

The Eagles last disciplined a player for conduct detrimental in 2001. In that case, three players were suspended without pay for one game for being taken into custody after police discovered marijuana in the car in which they were riding. The Eagles took the position that my interview, inappropriate apology, $150 late fine, attire for road games, parking, and the fight were worth eight hundred thousand dollars and an indefinite suspension, but that the other three players deserved only a one-game suspension for their alleged illegal misconduct. So, to their way of thinking, my speech in the interview was worse than their marijuana arrest.

My attorneys compared my situation to other cases. In August 2003, an Oakland Raiders linebacker initiated a fight with a teammate by ripping off his helmet and punching him in the face. The linebacker's vicious attack broke the bone around his teammate's left eye. The punch injured him so severely that he had to be put on injured reserve for the rest of the season and never played again. The linebacker's punishment was a fine that was a fraction of mine. He was disciplined by having to miss one day of training camp. So my calling the Eagles classless and agreeing with Michael Irvin that our record would be better if Brett Favre were our quarterback, especially since Donovan was hampered by nagging injuries, was, according to the Eagles, a greater offense than punching a teammate and ruining his career. Does that seem fair?

Okay, let's go to another situation. A Carolina Panthers receiver punched his teammate and was suspended without pay for one game. The same thing happened to two Cincinnati Bengals. A Chargers receiver not only beat up his teammate but also verbally assaulted his coach, which almost caused them to get into a fight. On the other hand, I was the one who almost got punched in the eye; Hugh threw a punch that could have ruined my career. And I was the one being disciplined? I was the one who was supposed to apologize three different times? Are you kidding me? This is why the legal experts familiar with NFL case law all predicted a landslide victory for me in this case.

Let's keep going here. A Saints player was initially fined $88,000 because he walked off the field during a game after arguing with a coach. After looking at the CBA requirements and the case precedent, the arbitrator reduced the fine from $88,000 to $5,000. Another Saints player was initially suspended for one game without pay amounting to $18,600 for refusing to practice after arguing with a coach. The arbitrator there reduced the fine to $2,000 because the arbitrator found the coach had some responsibility for the escalation, and the team didn't prove just cause for the discipline it imposed. A Cleveland Browns player was fined $46,000 by the team for demanding to be traded and refusing to practice; the Browns claimed that his refusal to practice caused a disruption and that he tried to sabotage their practices. The arbitrator reduced the fine from $46,000 to $200 because the Browns could not prove that it was intentional sabotage. Again, these are precedents that establish what the discipline should be. How was I supposed to know that my remarks in an interview after being attacked by Hugh constituted an offense so much worse than punching a teammate and ending his career, or refusing to practice, or quitting during a game that I should be fined $800,000 and suspended for the maximum games allowed, then deactivated for the remainder of the season? I might have caused a big stir with the media, but again, my conduct didn't compare to any of those acts.

My legal defense team also pointed to cases in the NBA, NHL, and Major League Baseball. Recently, in the NBA, several Indiana Pacers players jumped into the stands and started attacking Detroit Pistons fans. This was a huge story. One player was suspended for thirty games (37 percent of the season) and another player for fifteen games (18 percent of the season). My suspension and deactivation punished me for 56 percent of the season.

One NHL player punched an opponent, broke the guy's neck, and probably ended the man's career. His punishment was a thirteen-game suspension that was only 16 percent of the season. Another hockey player was suspended for twenty-three games (28 percent of the season) after being convicted of assault for hitting another NHL player in the face with his hockey stick. So according to the Eagles, my remarks in that interview were a worse offense and therefore deserved far more severe punishment than if I had punched a fan, a teammate, or another player. Was my exercise of speech at home more detrimental than their violent, career-ending attacks in games and at practice? What can possibly be more ridiculous than that? This is still America, right?

Let's take another case that involves just speech. A Major League Baseball pitcher drew fire for some really nasty comments. These are some of the things he had to say:

> So many dumb asses don't know how to drive in this town. . . . Look! Look at this idiot! I guarantee you she's a Japanese woman. How bad are Asian women at driving?

> Imagine having to take the [Number] 7 train to the ballpark [in New York], looking like you're [riding through] Beirut next to

some kid with purple hair next to some queer with AIDS right next to some dude who just got out of jail for the fourth time right next to some 20-year-old man with four kids. It's depressing.

The biggest thing I don't like about New York are the foreigners. I'm not a very big fan of foreigners . . . Asians and Koreans and Vietnamese and Indians and Russians and Spanish people and everything up there. How the hell did they get in this country?

He also called an overweight black teammate "a fat monkey."

The pitcher's racist, derogatory, offensive remarks insulted the entire world, including his teammates. Any fair person would have to agree that what I said was nothing compared to what he said. His punishment was a suspension that got reduced to a two-week suspension during training camp and another two weeks during the regular season *with pay*. He was fined five hundred dollars. I, on the other hand, was fined eight hundred thousand dollars and was being forced to miss most of the season. To argue that my statements deserved much more severe punishment than his just shows how unfair the Eagles were being toward me.

Looking at what the other disciplined players did, and at the punishment they received, it was clear to every legal expert that the Eagles' position was absurd.

To close out the legal argument, Kessler and Berthelsen made two more points. First, the Eagles were required to discipline me in a progressive manner. They hadn't done this. Second, for due-process reasons, the Eagles were required to conduct some type of investigation into the fight before disciplining me, and they never once asked me what happened. I had a right to state my case to my employer before being disciplined for the fight. In fact, Hugh testified that he immediately went up to Coach Reid's office and told him that he'd started the whole situation and threw the first punch. Hugh accepted the blame for what he did. After being told that their Team Ambassador started the fight and was responsible, the Eagles knew full well that I was the victim, yet they stated in their suspension letter to me that I was being disciplined for fighting with a team employee. Is that crazy or what? Then the letter was somehow anonymously released to the media to make it look as if I was the bad guy there.

Our case was so strong and so clear that the attorney for the Eagles focused most of his energy on contending that even if the arbitrator were to reverse the suspension, Coach Reid still had the authority to deactivate me for the rest of the season so long as I got paid. The issue had become not whether the Eagles were going to lose but how badly.

They tried very hard to make the point that Arbitrator Bloch lacked the authority to order Coach Reid to restore my status to where it was before the suspension. They were saying that nobody could force Coach Reid to let me participate in practice and be a part of the team again, no matter how unfairly I'd been treated.

In a funny exchange, Jeff pointed out in plain English exactly where in the CBA it said that the arbitrator has that precise authority. Whether Bloch could go so far as to state that I had to be put into a game was another matter. At the very least, Jeff made it clear I was entitled to practice, attend meetings, and work out at the facility just like any other player on the team.

The big question was, what were the Eagles going to be required to do once my suspension was reversed? Would they be allowed to deactivate me for the remainder of the season, or would they be forced to either play me or release me?

After we all emerged from the thirteen-hour-long hearing, the speculation was that once the Eagles lost the case they were going to release me. Although my attorneys still cautioned me that anything was possible, they knew the hearing could not have gone better. While I was still nervous about the fact that Bloch was so indifferent toward me and so friendly toward Coach Reid, I was confident he would do his job and make his decision in accordance with the CBA and case precedent.

Before Bloch concluded the meeting, he told us he would have a decision by Monday or Tuesday. I walked out of there without making any comment to the media. Jeff Kessler, who normally keeps a low profile, was so confident that he addressed the media with the following comment: "The discipline did not meet the legal standards of the collective bargaining agreement. . . . He wants to play for Philadelphia. He doesn't have any problem with his teammates, the organization, or the fans. He never expected this to be the result."

As I drove off, I looked at Jeff being surrounded by the cameras and felt satisfied with the way things went, even though it was painful to be on opposite sides of the table from the team I had given so much to the year before. Still, I felt an overall sense of vindication, felt that there was going to be justice for me this time, not just for everyone else.

18

The Perfect Crime

ALTHOUGH it was extremely stressful to wait four days until Tuesday for Bloch's decision, I tried to stay relaxed. I realized that Tuesday would be soon enough for a decision, because the real practice for the week starts on Wednesday.

Over the weekend, the Eagles lost again and their record was 4–6. I didn't watch the game because it would have been too frustrating not to be out there with my teammates, but I was disappointed they lost. I wanted the team to be 5–5 when I came back so we could be in position to catch up. Nevertheless, the season wasn't lost, and I believed with all my heart that we would turn things around. Bringing a Super Bowl victory to the fans of Philadelphia was still my vision.

When Tuesday came, Drew was with me as we were expecting the call. When his phone rang and we saw it was my attorneys on the line, we stood there in total anticipation. But the word was that we were going to have to wait one more day.

Why? I was told the cause of the delay was that Bloch needed more time. I had my doubts about that and wondered if he had an ulterior motive for keeping the world in suspense awaiting his ruling. I didn't think it was a good sign, but every expert and their mother still predicted the suspension was going to be reduced to one or two games.

At that point, I had spoken with a lot of teammates, and they said that almost all the guys wanted me to come back.

Even if the suspension were reversed, the question was what would happen next. We wanted the Eagles to either play me or release me so I could go somewhere else. We were ready to file another grievance if we had to, but we hoped it would be unnecessary.

My plan was to talk to Coach Reid and tell him once more that I would smooth things over with Donovan. I was prepared to do what it took to get back on track with the Eagles. That was my first choice. I really didn't want to go somewhere else that season. I was very excited at the idea of playing with Mike McMahon to help the team win the Super Bowl. I believed with total confidence we could do that.

The next morning, Bob Glauber, a reporter for *Newsday,* wrote that Bloch had decided to reduce my suspension to one or two games and I would be immediately reinstated. Eagles insiders such as ESPN's Sal Paolantonio reported that if the suspension was reduced as expected, the Eagles were likely to release me. Although I wanted to stay with the Eagles, most of all I wanted to play and would go wherever the best opportunity presented itself.

I was already looking forward to holding a press conference and thanking my legal team of Richard Berthelsen, Jeff Kessler, David Feher, Adam Kaiser, and David Greenspan for an outstanding effort on my behalf.

Around midafternoon Drew got the call we were waiting for from Jeff Kessler. We were all excited. And then on speaker, I heard Jeff tell Drew that we had lost, we had lost on everything. It sounded like a prank call. It seemed like a bad joke.

Jeff was beside himself with shock and anger. He was so upset he could barely talk. I could not believe what happened had really happened. How could we lose? Didn't Bloch have to decide by the rules? Could he just do whatever he wanted? How could something so unfair be final? Wasn't there anything I could do? Am I really barred from playing for the rest of the season? How could this happen? This can't be real. There must be something I can do.

The reality was there was nothing I could do to fight it. I decided to get some air and think things through.

When I had cooled down a little, I talked to Jason Rosenhaus about the logistics of Bloch's decision.

As an attorney and CPA himself, Jason was able to talk legalese with the attorneys, but he could also translate a fifty-page document or an hour-long legal discussion into a five-minute explanation whenever I needed him to. I sat next to Jason throughout the arbitration hearing, and when the decision came down, I wanted Jason to review it with me.

Jason showed me the beginning of Bloch's decision, which stated:

> For the reasons to be discussed, the findings are (1) the four-week suspension was for just cause and (2) there was no contract violation inherent in Club's determining that Owens should not return to the team. Resolution of this dispute requires recognition of *the highly unusual nature of this case,* the existing boundaries of applicable CBA language and, above all, *a clear understanding of the facts.*

The one phrase that said it all was "the highly unusual nature of this case." With those words, Bloch declared his intention to make a decision based on what he thought of me and my alleged actions, and not on the precedents, the meaning of the CBA, or the bounds of normal labor law.

The decision spent a significant amount of space on my conduct during the off-season and training camp, and the letters the Eagles sent to me at the time. I guess the "highly unusual nature" meant that concepts like double jeopardy and the forty-five-day rule for discipline don't apply to me, just to everybody else in the NFL. That's pretty disturbing.

Even more disturbing, in discussing the supposedly disruptive influence of my comments in the ESPN.com interview, he wrote, "Ultimately, the import of this, and similar remarks, has not so much to do with its actual content as it does with the potential and reasonably predictable impact on others, including McNabb."

So, according to Bloch, the standard for permitted speech by a player is not what he says but whether there are predictable consequences. Before talking to the media, we have to think through all possible angles of what the media might do with the story. And two players can say exactly the same thing, but if one of them causes a stir with the media, that player's conduct is detrimental. That's not exactly the uniform standard required by the CBA.

Throughout, Bloch argued that my actions constituted an unbroken string of disruptions and attacks on the team and on Donovan in particular. He completely ignored the way I toned everything down once I returned to training camp determined to make the best of things. At one point, he wrote, "Faced, as it was, with growing, palpable evidence of a disturbed and distracted team, *a media storm that continued to be aided and abetted by the Player,* and an apparent inability or unwillingness on the part of Mr. Owens to appreciate the destructive impact of his attitude and the jeopardy that surrounded him, the Club would reasonably take the actions it did."

I "aided and abetted" a media storm? How, exactly, did I do that—by not talking to the media? By saying positive things in the vast majority of my few public remarks? According to Bloch, I was responsible for all the talk and speculation that swirled around me and around my situation on the team: "Terrell Owens' stature as a compelling athlete and outspoken public figure contributed meaningfully to the destructive power of his actions." So it's not the actions themselves but the results of those actions, fueled by my reputation for controversy, that made it okay for the Eagles to keep me out of football for the rest of the season. So much for uniform standards. So much for equal treatment.

The final issue in Bloch's decision was whether the Eagles had the right to send me home for as long as they wanted despite the maximum-punishment rule, and whether it was an unfair punishment in relation to the offense. Bloch wrote that the first issue was a conflict between the CBA's maximum-discipline provision and the coach's authority to decide which players take the field.

The NFLPA's position was that they either had to practice me and treat me like everyone else on the team or release me. After noting that the events of this case were "highly unique," Bloch wrote that "one may not claim that mere professional disadvantage to a player withheld from play or practice is necessarily disciplinary action as contemplated under Article VIII. Recognizing there may be situations that touch both the disciplinary and the discretionary arenas, what counts are the precise circumstances at issue."

Jason explained to me that this may have been the most astonishing thing in the decision. With this sentence, Bloch reversed a landmark decision of his own, that whether an action constitutes punishment is based on its substance, not its form. Here he made the argument that sending me home, preventing me from practicing my trade, and barring me from playing the game that I love is not punishment. To qualify his absurd position, Bloch wrote the disclaimer that "what counts are the precise circumstances at issue." So, basically, because the circumstances pertained to me instead of everyone else, the CBA and all the other rights afforded to every NFL player didn't apply. Talk about a double standard!

Bloch then wrote and italicized the words as follows: "This case, then, is about the challenge faced by *this* team, dealing with *this* player in *these particular circumstances.*"

Bloch excused his deviation from the CBA, established labor law principles, and NFL case precedent by stating that his ruling was unique to me. How can this happen? How can the collectively bargained right of all players to be treated equally just be thrown out the window?

For Bloch to conclude that "both responses, the disciplinary and the discretionary, were specifically understood by these parties" is just wrong. I never understood or was informed that I could possibly be disciplined for more than one game, let alone the remaining nine games.

Bloch's last words were that the suspension was for just cause and that the deactivation was not a violation of the CBA "due to the nature of [my] conduct and its destructive and continuing threat to the team."

With that decision, Arbitrator Richard Bloch's own conduct became a destructive and continuing threat to the CBA that the NFLPA would need to address. The man robbed me without a gun! It was the perfect crime.

I was hardly the only one who was shocked. Len Pasquarelli, who is probably the most respected journalist in sports, wrote in his column for ESPN.com:

> "It was even better than we thought it might be," said one Philadelphia management official, trying hard not to gloat too much, Wednesday afternoon.
>
> Truth be told, here's what the Eagles figured as their best-case scenario, as they assessed Bloch's options: The arbitrator would uphold the four-game suspension but order that the

team permit Owens to report back to work after Sunday's game against Green Bay, the final week the franchise was allowed to sanction him under the parameters of the catch-all charge of "conduct detrimental to the team." And then, forced to have Owens back at the facility, lifting weights and on the practice field, the team would have to decide whether to keep him around as an expensive "scout team" player or simply release him.

There it is in black and white. Not even the Eagles were expecting Bloch to rule in their favor.

The NFL released a statement that they were pleased with the decision. Why would the NFL be pleased to lose one of its biggest stars? Wouldn't you think they'd want us to work out some kind of compromise? I guess the league's statement alone shows the division between the league and its players. I thank God that the players have Gene Upshaw and NFLPA president Troy Vincent looking out for them.

That was why the NFLPA was so angry with this decision. A "shocked" Richard Berthelsen had this comment on Bloch's decision: "I think the arbitrator chose to accept not only the Eagles' version of the evidence, but I think he went even further and pieced the evidence together in a way that it really didn't evolve. He describes all of the events leading up to the suspension, but ignored the fact that Terrell was a model citizen from the week he was gone in training camp until Nov. 3. If you view, as [Bloch] did, the one week [Reid] sent [Owens] home as a form of discipline, that wiped out all prior conduct.

"We are obviously very disappointed with Arbitrator Bloch's decision. His ruling . . . ignores the obligation a club has to either provide employment to a player or allow him to play somewhere else. We are confident that we put on a winning case at the hearing last Friday, and we still believe Terrell Owens had a right to a legitimate reinstatement."

Gene Upshaw took it one step further with his reaction: "One thing I can control is that he will no longer be an arbitrator in any more of our cases. Under the [Collective Bargaining Agreement], either side has a right between Dec. 1 and Dec. 10 to dismiss an arbitrator, and we are going to dismiss this one." And that's exactly what the NFLPA did.

By the time Bloch's decision came in, the Philadelphia Eagles fans and almost all of the players wanted me back. Coach Reid himself struggled with the decision at the midnight hour.

The TV networks would have done cartwheels to see me come back and play for the Eagles. Imagine if I'd been able to help Mike McMahon be successful at quarterback. It could have happened. How exciting would that have been? The fans would have loved it.

Unfortunately, the people with the power were against it, and everybody lost. Did the Eagles win? No, they went on to finish 6–10, their worst season in a long time. Did the NFL win? No, they lost out on what would have been a thrilling story that the fans and the networks would have loved. Did the fans win? Definitely not; they would have loved to root for me or against me. Did I lose? In the short run, yes, because I lost nine chances to play the game I love in front of my fans and family.

All of that was painful to accept, but here's what I did not lose: my dignity! I paid a steep price for it, but I can look at myself in the mirror and respect who I am. I stood up for myself and fought back. I know I'm a better person for all of this. The next time I step onto that field, I will have more love and appreciation for the game that was taken away from me. Things happen for a reason. I have learned a great deal from this experience, and I have a better understanding of what to say to the media and what not to say.

That was why I wanted to write this book. I held my

tongue after Bloch's decision came in and for many months thereafter. I knew that no matter what I said, the media and critics of the world would spin it, and the fans would get a distorted perspective. Every time I apologized, some commentator would come in and take a small piece of what I had to say and would present it as if it were the whole thing. These so-called experts said this and that about whether I was sincere and what they thought; they took their shots at me and never really let the public hear what I was saying.

When a report on *SportsCenter* or your local newspaper gives you a sentence that I've said, they're reporting a fact—that is something I said. But when that sentence is taken out of context, when the report skips over all the positive things I've had to say to pull out the one negative thing that gives them a headline, well, that may be a fact but it isn't the truth.

I wrote this book so that you, the reader, can get the real me straight from me and can decide for yourself what kind of person I am. If anyone in the media dares to say that this was just a money-making scheme and that I just signed my name to someone else's words, then that's a vindication right there of what I am talking about. That person has no idea about any of the facts surrounding this book and is making false accusations, out of complete ignorance of or disregard for the truth. I expect the media will do just that, count on it. For the record, this was my idea and is my story—no one else's.

Now, all that aside, I believe that any person who reads this with an open mind will see I made my share of mistakes—but everyone deserves a second chance. I want to be the MVP—the most valuable player, not the most vilified player. Maybe football fans will understand my perspective and why I did what I did. You don't have to like me, but at least respect the fact that I had my reasons. Don't let the media or people who didn't read this tell you anything different from the conclusions you've drawn after reading my story. The media don't get the chance to come between us as you read this. This time it is just you and me.

I believe my case was Bloch's last case as a sports arbitrator. The NFLPA dismissed him specifically because of this decision. A little while later, I found out that he's no longer an arbitrator for Major League Baseball either. Perhaps he can fill any holes in his schedule with his sideline: He's also a professional magician. He must be good; he certainly made all my rights disappear.

19
Moving On

So now I had to accept the fact that my 2005 season was over. I had to get through six more weeks of the regular season, the playoffs, the Super Bowl, and then the off-season to make it to the start of free agency on March 3. At times it was a battle, but I tried to keep busy and productive by training hard to stay in top condition and having a little bit of fun along the way.

With my birthday falling a few weeks after the ruling, my publicist, Kim, threw me a birthday party at a nightclub in Atlantic City on Monday, December 12. It was a fun time for everybody—except for the media, who showed up hoping that Drew or I would comment on my situation, which neither of us did. But my friends and teammates had a blast.

I'm not much of a socializer, but the few friends I make, I keep. They were all there to support me, as were most of my family. My good friend Michael Irvin joined us in the VIP section and led the crowd in singing "Happy Birthday." Drew; Jason; my marketing agent, Robert Bailey; my financial advisor, Jeff Rubin, and his associate, Matt Cassano; and Drew's new hire, Danny Martoe, all joined in on the fun.

A lot of my teammates showed up to support me as well. The Eagles who came included Jevon Kearse, Jerome

McDougle, Brian Westbrook, Lito Sheppard, Todd Pinkston, L. J. Smith, Shawn Andrews, Trent Cole, Hollis Thomas, N. D. Kalu, and about ten others, and everybody had a fun time. Other NFL players from around the league who came were Washington Redskins Pro Bowl running back Clinton Portis and Cleveland Browns running back Reuben Droughns. Although I invited Donovan, he didn't make it.

With music playing in the background, I took the microphone and made my first public remarks since my suspension. I said that I loved the city of Philadelphia, the fans, and my teammates. I had nothing negative to say about anyone. While I was speaking, there was a rap song in the background, and I reiterated what the rapper was rapping: "I ain't never going to let anyone change me." Afterward, the media made that into something, when it was really nothing.

Kim did a great job with the party, and everybody there had an awesome time. When asked about my loving comments, Kim said, "That's the side of Terrell that unfortunately people who aren't close to him don't get to see. That's how he is when he's in his element, surrounded by family and friends."

Eagles tight end L. J. Smith told the media, "Personally, he never did anything to me. He invited the whole team. That says a lot. He's a great teammate." Jevon Kearse described me as "a wonderful teammate," and when asked if he was worried that management would be upset with him for coming to my party, he answered, "Last time I checked, I'm an adult."

As Andy Reid acknowledged, I do have a lot of friends on the team. I was very happy they showed up to support me. My party wasn't about sending some kind of message to the Eagles, it was about me and my teammates being together and having a great time. The night was all about friends getting together, and we popped the champagne and celebrated.

The rest of the year and the beginning of 2006 went well for me, considering the circumstances. I didn't talk to the media, I trained hard to stay in top shape, and I was ready for the free-agency process to begin. I felt that I had made it through the woods and was emerging as a hot commodity.

Shortly after the Denver Broncos lost in the playoffs, their head coach, Mike Shanahan, invited Drew and me over to his house in Denver. The Eagles had given me permission to seek a trade, and we took advantage of that opportunity to have a face to face with Coach Shanahan.

I thought the meeting went very well. I talked about what had happened and told him how I'd like things to go this upcoming season with my new team. I'm not much of a salesman, but I wanted him to see that I honestly wanted to have a great year on the field and in the locker room with my new teammates. Coach Shanahan responded well to what I had to say and expressed an interest in me playing for him next season.

When word broke that I had met with him, the media ran with the story as expected. Shortly thereafter, word got out that the Kansas City Chiefs were interested in me as well. My stock was up and everything was very positive as I headed into free agency. Other than the Super Bowl, the big story in late January and early February was what teams were interested in me and to what degree. Things were going in the right direction, and I was going to hit the free market at long last.

As everything was looking good, and I put the past behind me, I was completely blindsided by the timing of an interview that Donovan gave that was published on February 1. Maybe it was just a coincidence that he was being interviewed about my situation as my free agency was coming into play. For some reason, he wanted to rehash the past.

Donovan came clean and said that everything was fine between us until the Giants game in 2004. His version of what happened was:

Not a lot of people would know about this because [Owens] had a great season, everything went well, everybody's smiling and enjoying themselves, but I believe it was the third play of the game. We had an "all-go" call, [I] dropped back five steps, looked downfield, at that time I didn't feel he came open, and checked it down to Brian Westbrook. It was an incomplete pass.

I thought it interesting that he brought the Giants game up now after ignoring it for so long. Donovan continued with what happened after the play:

He came back, "Hey, I was open, throw the ball!" Me being into the game, [I said], "Hey, get in the huddle, man." In different words, obviously. He continued to talk about how he was open, throw the ball. And it [led] to me using some language that's really not suitable for the kids. But I'm into the game. *I'm running the huddle. This is my show.* I'm going to see you a lot of plays and some plays I won't see you. That led to us talking in the locker room. I don't argue. *I feel as men we can talk.* Voices are going to get raised. But we can talk as men and when the conversation is over we understand each other [emphasis added].

First, I said the following seven words to him and only these seven words in the huddle: "Dude, I was open, you missed me." I didn't go on and on. Then to say, "This is my show," makes it pretty clear that he was threatened by my presence. Finally, his saying, "I feel as men we can talk," is a joke. I went to talk to him like a man in the locker room, and rather than make things right between us he acted confrontational and when I didn't back down, he just walked away. He didn't mention that in the interview, did he?

Donovan's version of what happened next:

I called him a couple of days later just to get back on the same page. I just elaborated to him, "Hey, if we're going to continue to do this, we're not going anywhere. We have to be on the same page. I brought you here for a reason, for people to understand the chemistry that we have and the things we can do, which will lead us to winning a Super Bowl."

He did call me a couple of days later, but he didn't try to smooth things over, he just tried to explain to me that he was the boss. I didn't care for that. To hear him say to me, "I brought you here for a reason," as if he was in charge, instead of Andy Reid or Joe Banner, was ridiculous. Last time I checked he wasn't the head coach.

Why did Donovan and I fall out? I think Donovan reveals the truth without even knowing it. When asked to explain what happened, Donovan answered:

> It was money and power. Obviously, with the whole money situation I have no control over that. That's between that individual and the organization. And the whole power situation of being the face of the team or the recognizable guy—*if it's that he was trying to outdo me* or outdo the organization, whatever—that's what I felt led to what's been going on [emphasis added].

I think that was the root of problem—Donovan's misperception that I was trying to outdo him. I was very respectful and had nothing but praise for Donovan. Remember before the Giants game, when I told the media, "My Thanksgiving came in March when I got to be with Donovan"? I think I was a pretty good teammate during that whole 2004 season. It wasn't my fault that I got the lion's share of attention that used to go to him. I wasn't trying to overshadow Donovan; I was just being me and it happened on its own.

ESPN reporter Sal Paolantonio wrote, "When Owens showed up in Philadelphia, he didn't follow the unwritten rules of the Andy Reid way. No, Owens flaunted his style and name—from overshadowing Donovan McNabb in training camp, to mocking Ray Lewis, the Ravens' revered middle linebacker."

That was the problem, right there.

Further along in the interview, Donovan insisted he wasn't tired in the Super Bowl, even though in his comments right after the game he said that he was. But what really got to me was how he treated my comments about Brett Favre. What Donovan said must have shocked most of the sports world, but I already knew that side of Donovan.

I said in my interview with Graham Bensinger that I agreed with ESPN analyst Michael Irvin's assessment that the Eagles would be undefeated if Brett Favre were the quarterback. The point was that Donovan was banged up, which was no secret. I wasn't the one who selected Brett Favre for comparison, Michael Irvin was. Donovan's response to my statement:

> In that situation, it was kinda like, "That's unreal." That's just like me saying, "If we had Steve Largent, if we had Joe Jurevicius we'd be undefeated." He'll now have to answer the question for the whole week about me saying it.

ESPN's Michael Smith, who conducted the interview with Donovan, wrote, "McNabb's selection of two white receivers was not by accident. He took Owens' choice of Favre as disrespectful to McNabb as an African-American quarterback."

Donovan went on to tell Smith:

> It was definitely a slap in the face to me. Because as deep as people won't go into it, it was [a] black-on-black crime.
>
> And to say if we had Brett Favre, that could mean that if you

had another quarterback of a different descent or ethnic background, we could be winning. That's something I thought
about and said, "Wow." It's different to say if we had Michael
Vick, Daunte Culpepper, Steve McNair, Aaron Brooks, Byron
Leftwich. But to go straight to Brett Favre, that slapped me in
the face, like what I've done and what I set out to do.

But for me to see that, that shows that you have a problem
with me. Is it jealousy? The commercials I'm in? Me being the
franchise quarterback?

Wow! Now I was insulted. Not only did he accuse me of
being a bad teammate, but now I was racist, too. That was
too ridiculous to merit a response.

Am I supposed to believe that he wouldn't have been insulted if I'd mentioned a black quarterback on another team
who wasn't as good? That would have been an even bigger
slap in the face! I was talking about future Hall of Famer Brett
Favre. What does race have to do with anything I said?

Anyway, I didn't pick Brett Favre, Irvin did. As smooth and
talented as Donovan is in front of the camera, not even he
could sell that I was being racist here. I simply agreed with my
black friend Michael and tried to defend Donovan by saying
our record would also be better if Donovan were healthy.
Somehow Donovan turned that into a "black-on-black crime."

Up until the Giants game, I praised Donovan every chance
I got. For him to say, "Is it jealousy?" I think reveals how he
himself was feeling.

Smith asked Donovan about my party, and whether it was
disrespectful for teammates to come to it, and to lobby for my
reinstatement after Donovan went down with his injuries. He
said:

It bothered me. Not about the party situation, because a
party's a party. It bothered me when you hear, "He didn't do

anything personal to me." It bothered me when teammates say, "We can't win without him." It bothered me in that situation because you're not showing confidence in the guys that are out there. . . . Nobody took any pride in it to say, with all that's going on, is this killing our season? And answer it yourself.

Look, I didn't kill the Eagles' season. I believe I could have made a difference and helped Mike McMahon. We could have kept ourselves in the hunt, but Coach Reid decided not to bring me back at the midnight hour when it could have gone either way. While Donovan "suggested" that the team "might be better off" without me, history proved otherwise. The guys wanted to win and they wanted me back. I didn't see anything wrong with that.

Donovan on the other hand did. He viewed taking me back as an affront to his control of the team. When asked if he took his teammates' showing support for me as a stab in the back, he answered:

It put something in the back of my mind that you really learn a lot about people when things aren't going good. Comments, answers to questions, reactions—you learn about people. I'm not here to call any players out. They know who they are. With this whole interview, people will see that we really need to evaluate the situation. For [Owens] to talk about me, for him to talk about the organization, think about what actually just happened. That's the message I'd like to send. Why is it that we have to go back to the team that we were in 2001, 2002, 2003, 2004, why say we have to get back to the camaraderie we had when we should have done it this year?

That nobody really came to my defense, that showed me a lot. That nobody came out to say he's wrong in the media when somebody asks you a question, it was like, "That's his situation, that's between them, his contract, I think Donovan has handled it well . . ." Come out and say, "It should not have happened. That was wrong. This is Donovan's team." Again, I'll always remember what happened. Two-thousand-five was a beautiful year.

I don't care what anyone says, once the season started, I put my own issues aside and worked as hard as I could to win. I played very well and kept my teammates out of what was going on between Donovan and me. I didn't ask anyone to take up for me and I didn't want anyone else to get involved. I wasn't trying to make it my team.

What in the world was so beautiful about 2005? I thought it was a terrible year—the Eagles had a losing season, he got hurt, and I got suspended. There was nothing beautiful about it. Was it beautiful because he learned which of his teammates did not go out of their way to get involved in something that was not their business? Is that a threat to his teammates? What kind of leader is that?

Columnist Vin Diec on the website Sports Column wrote after the interview:

Why not just confront Owens? Why is the onus on the other guy to come talk to you, Donovan? Shouldn't the leader of the team be the one that gets into people's faces? Marino never had a problem doing that. Steve Young never had a problem doing that. McNabb thinks that by throwing the ball into Owens' court, it absolves him of any responsibility for the situation. Donovan assumes that he's taking the high road but sometimes, the high road isn't the right road. I'm not defending Owens here because, clearly, TO is a petulant child that needs to corralled. What was needed from "5" was that he put TO in line but, unfortunately, McNabb wasn't the person to do it and it "divided the team" (Donovan's words). . . .

You can blame TO all you want for tearing apart the Eagles season and potentially the franchise for years to come. But in the end, you must also blame McNabb, the self-proclaimed leader who shows very little in the way of leadership. Donovan thought it was a good time to air his side of the story and elicit sympathy for his cause. Unfortunately, all it did was expose his flaws.

In the end, it all comes down to Andy Reid, who has tried to make McNabb into something he is not, but that is another column.

Exactly. I accept that I played a role in tearing apart the Eagles' season, but the blame was not all mine.

In the end, Coach Reid was right about one thing: I focused too much on Donovan's negatives. With the passing of 2005, I let all that negativity go. I even had some concerns about writing this book. I was very uncomfortable discussing what went on behind closed doors.

Most of the incidents I've talked about here have been in the media already. What hasn't been told is my side. That's why I wrote this book. I wanted my fans and everyone who has an interest in me to know what really happened and why. I don't ever expect to be elected mayor of Philadelphia, but I hope that the kids out there who cheered for me won't have any hard feelings. I said that I love the city of Philadelphia, and I really mean it. When I have to play against the Eagles this season, it will be with a heavy heart.

20
My Turn

I **WAITED** what seemed like an eternity for the start of free agency. The signing period was scheduled to begin on the first day of the league year, which was Friday, March 3, 2006. My contract with the Eagles had a roster bonus clause that would pay me $5 million if I was on the team's roster on the fifth day of the 2006 league year. To avoid having to pay me that money, the Eagles needed to release me on the fourth day, which should have been on Monday, March 6. I couldn't wait.

Free agency doesn't begin with the business morning of the first day, it starts at 12:01 A.M., when the calendar turns. So that Thursday afternoon, I was watching the clock until midnight to begin my five-day countdown. But for some strange reason, when it's my turn for free agency, there has to be drama.

There was a major contract negotiation going on between the league owners and the NFLPA, with huge ramifications for the upcoming free-agent season. The CBA was set to expire at midnight March 2, and without an extension, the salary cap was going to be approximately $94.5 million. There were restrictions involved that would make it hard for teams without much cap room to get deals done at a reasonable salary-cap cost. A new CBA extension would add about $8 million to the salary cap and remove a lot of the restrictions on the structure of contracts.

There was a lot on the line for me and every other player awaiting his shot at free agency. On Thursday afternoon, the situation leaked bleak. I saw Richard Berthelsen and Jeff Kessler comment to ESPN that the negotiations were "dead as a doornail" and that the NFL "was unwilling to compromise."

They looked like men on a mission. I knew that with those two at the bargaining table alongside Gene Upshaw, we were going to win this time and get a great deal. I pictured those two relentlessly fighting for the players to get everything we deserved. I had every confidence that they were going to right what was wrong with the system.

I was not surprised at all when a few minutes later I saw that the owners and the NFLPA had agreed to extend the deadline until Sunday evening. The terms of the extension were that if an agreement could not be reached, free agency would begin with a $94.5-million salary cap at 12:01 A.M. Monday.

As Sunday night approached, I saw Kessler and Berthelsen again on ESPN. Kessler said, "The players have made every effort to reach a fair compromise. The union and players need to go forward. I don't see any further talks unless they give us a reason to believe. . . . Anything is possible, but [the owners] have to change their offer, because we're not changing ours."

Next thing I knew, there was another extension, until Wednesday evening. What happened was that NFL Commissioner Paul Tagliabue saved the day by getting the NFLPA to agree to the extension with the understanding that the negotiations were over and Tagliabue would present the NFLPA's position for a final vote to the owners.

After a tremendous effort by the commissioner, the owners

accepted the deal Wednesday night. The new terms scheduled the start of the league year and free agency to begin at 12:01 A.M., Friday, March 10. The new salary cap figure was now set at $102 million. There were going to be teams with the cap room necessary to sign me to the kind of contract I was looking for.

Additionally, the new CBA has specific language in it to undo the damage done by Richard Bloch's decision in my case, so that being deactivated as a form of discipline will count toward the four-week maximum-discipline provision. There is also very specific, player-friendly language regarding progressive discipline and bonus forfeitures for discipline. I knew that Richard Berthelsen would correct the CBA to make things right for every player from here on. This was a major victory for the NFLPA.

When I think of the support that NFLPA president Troy Vincent gave me during my suspension, and the fantastic effort that Richard and Jeff made on my behalf during the hearing, I was happy to see them come out on top. Now it was my turn.

I knew some teams had the cap room to sign me to a big deal, but I didn't know who and for how much. It was hard to gauge my fair market value. Drew was confident that the big deal was out there, as was I, but every expert on ESPN was saying I was going to have to sign a one-year deal making the minimum with incentives to sweeten the deal.

I had been scheduled to make $8.3 million with the Eagles in 2006, $5.5 million in 2007, and $6.5 million in 2008. And the top experts in the business were now predicting that I was only going to get a salary of $810,000 this year. They said I would have to sign for that amount with no guaranteed signing bonus, but I could make millions more in incentives. The ESPN "insiders" also predicted that I wouldn't sign a new contract for a month, and that Drew would have to work the teams over very hard to get a better deal than the minimum plus incentives.

I had to wait until 4:00 P.M. Tuesday, the deadline for the Eagles to release me, to become a free agent and test the waters. The deadline was Tuesday because the start of the league year had been pushed to Saturday morning to give the teams more time to prepare. On Tuesday afternoon, I was in Atlanta with Kim. Drew called me to let me know that ESPN had just reported that I was released and officially a free agent. I was relieved, but not yet excited.

With so many people saying I had lost millions of dollars by getting released and would never make that money back, it would have been easy for me to stress out. But I had faith that things were going to work out for the best.

One of the reasons I was so confident was that, regardless of the controversy surrounding my career, throughout it all my quarterbacks and I had had great success together. In fact, from 1999 through 2003 Jeff Garcia put up some very impressive numbers, which were comparable to Donovan's.

In 1999, both players were rookies. Jeff played in thirteen games and Donovan in twelve. As a rookie, Jeff threw eleven touchdowns, eleven interceptions, and 2,544 yards, putting together a quarterback rating of 77.9; Donovan threw eight touchdowns, seven interceptions, just 948 yards, and had only a 60.1 rating.

In 2000, both players became full-season starters. Jeff threw thirty-one touchdowns, ten interceptions, 4,278 yards, and put up a 97.6 rating. Donovan threw twenty-one touchdowns, thirteen interceptions, 3,365 yards, and improved his rating to 77.8.

The next season, in 2001, both players made the Pro Bowl. Jeff threw thirty-two touchdowns compared to Donovan's twenty-five. Jeff and Donovan both had twelve interceptions. Jeff put up 3,538 yards to Donovan's 3,233. Jeff's quarterback rating was 94.8 versus Donovan's 84.3.

Jeff made the Pro Bowl again in 2002, which was Donovan's best year statistically before I showed up. That year, Jeff completed twenty-one touchdowns, had ten interceptions, totaled 3,344 yards, and had a quarterback rating of 85.6. Donovan, having missed six games that year, threw seventeen touchdowns, had six interceptions, totaled 2,289 yards, and had a career-high rating at the time of 86.0.

In 2003, my last year with the 49ers, Jeff made the Pro Bowl once again, becoming a three-time consecutive Pro Bowler. Even though Jeff missed three games that season, his numbers were eighteen touchdowns, thirteen interceptions, 2,704 yards, and an 80.1 rating. Donovan's numbers were sixteen touchdowns, eleven interceptions, 3,216 yards, and a rating of 79.6.

In 2004, Donovan and I teamed up for a fantastic season. Donovan took it to a whole new level, throwing thirty-one touchdowns with only eight interceptions. He nearly doubled his touchdowns while significantly reducing his interceptions. His quarterback rating jumped through the roof, from 79.6 to 104.7.

Numbers don't lie, and the tale these tell is very persuasive. I had to believe there was a team out there that wanted me to continue the success that I had previously had with Jeff and Donovan. I am a man of faith—faith in God and myself—and, when I needed it most, it kept me strong.

So when Tuesday came and went with no significant phone calls from any teams, I didn't even think about panicking. I was prepared for the difficult, month-long process that ESPN's reporters predicted I was in for. Still, I remained confident. I woke up Wednesday morning and exercised the whole afternoon without any word—and then the phone call that I was waiting for came.

It was Drew on the line, and he told me that things were heating up with several teams and numbers were on the table that I was looking for. Drew told me that he had talked with head coach Bill Parcells and vice president Stephen Jones of the Cowboys, and he thought that was going to be the best situation.

Now I was excited, but still reserved, because nothing was signed yet. By Saturday morning, though, we had an official agreement. The new deal was going to be for a term of three years, and I would make $10 million the first year. I would get the first $5 million immediately on signing, and the remaining $5 million as a salary during the season. The second season called for a roster bonus of $3 million and a $5-million salary. The third year of the contract also had a $3-million roster bonus but with a $4-million salary. The contract was front loaded and only for three years; that way I could renegotiate after two years or become a free agent again after year three.

The total from 2006 through 2008 was $25 million. That was more than the first three years of Randy Moss's contract. The first three years of my 2004 contract with the Eagles was $20,680,000. The 2006 through 2008 compensation under that contract with the Eagles would have amounted to $20,270,000. I beat my previous contract by almost $5 million over those three years.

When Jerry Jones flew into Atlanta and picked me up in his private jet, I was holding back tears. Jerry showed up with his wife, his son Jerry Jr., and a friend of Jerry Jr.'s. I was with my mother, Marilyn; my sister Sharmaine; my nephew Caleb; Kim; my close friend A.J.; and Drew. The jet had a big Cowboys star emblem on it, and was the nicest jet I had ever been in. It was decorated with pictures of the three Super Bowl trophies the team won in the 1990s as well as pictures of the great players on those teams such as Troy Aikman, Michael Irvin, and Emmitt Smith. Jerry Jones was returning from a vacation in the Caribbean with his family, and welcomed me and my family with open arms.

I couldn't believe and will never forget the sincerity, humility, and kindness he showed me. Here was perhaps the most famous and powerful NFL owner, and he couldn't have been more warm and down to earth.

As we sat across from each other on the jet, I watched this self-made multimillionaire tell me that this was one of the happiest days of his career. He told me we were both great competitors with a passion to win the Super Bowl this year. He talked about his close relationship with Michael Irvin and how Michael's strong recommendation went a long way in making the decision to sign me. He explained to me that he had had his share of ups and downs in his life; there were times when he first started with the Cowboys that he was vilified, and he knew what it was like to be treated like Darth Vader. Then he talked about his impoverished upbringing—how he had to worry about how he was going to pay his bills or make a loan payment—but said that life has a way of working out. He told me how eager he had been to succeed as a student, and that he called numerous successful businesspeople to make appointments to sit down and learn from them.

Jerry then stressed how important it is that I manage my money wisely and build a good foundation off the field in the Dallas community for when I retired. He told me about how his relationships with Michael and Emmitt are special. He then looked me in the eyes, with great emotion, and told me that he wanted that kind of special relationship with me.

At that moment, as I thought of all the heartache and hardship I'd gone through with the Eagles, hearing Jerry Jones tell me how happy he was to have me on the team, that we had a lot in common, and how much he wanted me to be a part of his family, I was overwhelmed with emotion and fought the tears back.

I thanked him from the bottom of my heart and told him how happy I was and that we were going to win together.

The whole plane ride was so emotional and happy, it was hard to believe it was real. When I signed the contract at the Cowboys' facility, I knew then that my worst nightmare had led to a dream come true.

At the press conference, when all was said and done, I hugged my mother, Kim, and Drew. They all stood by me. My family's love gave me the strength to persevere. Kim kept me on the right track. Drew delivered.

And so, my friends, when I put on that Cowboys uniform and step on that field, know that I am going to give everything I have to accomplish three goals: first, honor the tradition of the Cowboys star; second, make Jerry Jones, Stephen Jones, and Bill Parcells look like geniuses for believing in me; and third, make the Cowboys fans love me by going to Miami on February 4, 2007, and taking home a Super Bowl trophy to add to Jerry's collection.

And to those who aren't my friends, I say to you: Come over to the winning side!